# How — Guide to Tea

## 101 Tips to Learn about, Make, Drink, and Enjoy Tea for Everyday Tea Drinkers

## HowExpert with Jessica Kanzler

For more tips related to this topic, visit HowExpert.com/tea.

# Recommended Resources

- HowExpert.com – Quick 'How To' Guides on All Topics from A to Z by Everyday Experts.
- HowExpert.com/free – Free HowExpert Email Newsletter.
- HowExpert.com/books – HowExpert Books
- HowExpert.com/courses – HowExpert Courses
- HowExpert.com/clothing – HowExpert Clothing
- HowExpert.com/membership – HowExpert Membership Site
- HowExpert.com/affiliates – HowExpert Affiliate Program
- HowExpert.com/jobs – HowExpert Jobs
- HowExpert.com/writers – Write About Your #1 Passion/Knowledge/Expertise & Become a HowExpert Author.
- HowExpert.com/resources – Additional HowExpert Recommended Resources
- YouTube.com/HowExpert – Subscribe to HowExpert YouTube.
- Instagram.com/HowExpert – Follow HowExpert on Instagram.
- Facebook.com/HowExpert – Follow HowExpert on Facebook.

# Publisher's Foreword

Dear HowExpert Reader,

HowExpert publishes quick 'how to' guides on all topics from A to Z by everyday experts.

At HowExpert, our mission is to discover, empower, and maximize everyday people's talents to ultimately make a positive impact in the world for all topics from A to Z...one everyday expert at a time!

All of our HowExpert guides are written by everyday people just like you and me, who have a passion, knowledge, and expertise for a specific topic.

We take great pride in selecting everyday experts who have a passion, real-life experience in a topic, and excellent writing skills to teach you about the topic you are also passionate about and eager to learn.

We hope you get a lot of value from our HowExpert guides, and it can make a positive impact on your life in some way. All of our readers, including you, help us continue living our mission of positively impacting the world for all spheres of influences from A to Z.

If you enjoyed one of our HowExpert guides, then please take a moment to send us your feedback from wherever you got this book.

Thank you, and we wish you all the best in all aspects of life.

Sincerely,

BJ Min
Founder & Publisher of HowExpert
HowExpert.com

PS...If you are also interested in becoming a HowExpert author, then please visit our website at
HowExpert.com/writers. Thank you & again, all the best!

# Table of Contents

# Chapter 1: Knowing Your Tea

## *A Brief Introduction*

The first time I tasted tea, I was in a hotel room in Oregon. I was 8 years old, and my family was getting ready to make the last leg of our journey to a new home. My parents made coffee from the black plastic coffee maker the hotel had provided. I remember there being a little black tray that had a couple of little bags of coffee, sugar, and two other mysterious packets. Having learned to read not that long ago, I was excited to ask what "tea" was because that's all that was written on the front of the package. A white paper square, black text, "Tea."

My mom said something like, "It's good. You'll like it," and my dad laughed for some reason. I didn't understand, but I was enthralled seeing my mother bring a mug of water to a boil in the microwave and plop a fibrous bag into it. She told me to wait, and I passed the long minutes, which felt like hours to my impatient child-brain, staring at the steaming cup on the counter. It smelled weird, like coffee but not.

After a while, my mom said it was ready and handed me the cup, warning me that it was hot. It was, and I remember my hands tingling from the heat, but I didn't care. I was an adult now. I had a hot cup of something just like my parents. I'd have to tell my brother I'd get to ride in the front seat now that I was clearly the elder sibling—my cup, full of vaguely translucent brown liquid, steamed as if mirroring my anticipation. I took my first sip of tea.

And spat it out. Disgusting. Filth. Vile. Worse than the coffee my parents had let me try. Worse than the prune juice, I'd mistaken it for grape. Worse than anything.

Tea is a drink, and it is a plant, and from that plant, we can derive a wildly variable set of flavors that make up the second-most widely consumed beverage in the world, second only to water. Seeing a bag only labeled as tea is like saying you're going on vacation to "a place." While it may be technically true, there is a world of specificity missing.

Tea is as variable as the people who drink it, and while the lessons here will discuss a standard way of doing things for different teas, they are not rules. For many, tea is a cultural drink brewed and consumed in ceremonies. For others, it has significant personal and emotional value. Others still may see it only as an alternative to coffee. Tea changes with the person, and this text will seek to discuss the standard experiences that can be shared to create the best cup of tea possible. It does not account for nuances in personal taste. Some people may enjoy a more bitter concoction, and others may like their tea hot enough to make their upper lip numb just by drinking it. Your nuanced love for tea is still justified if it differs from some of the lessons contained here. Still, if you are looking for a place to start modifying how you consume this wonderfully variable beverage, you may find something interesting here.

While the plant that most teas come from, Camellia sinensis, originated in Southeast Asia, tea is now consumed across the world. There are many different types of tea to match the many cultures that consume it; some enjoyed it for its medicinal properties, some steeped in cultural value. Others used it as a source of caffeine easier on the body than coffee. There are many different types of tea, all with their own brewing needs, effects on the body, and unique flavor profiles. Tea is consumed all over the world, so to define and discuss every type of tea would take much more than one book, so to start, we can look at some of the most widely consumed types of tea: Green, Black, White, Oolong, and Herbal.

## *Green Tea*

Green tea is the closest you can get to plain tea. A tea bag could justifiably be only labeled as "tea" if it contained plain green tea. Green tea is made from leaves plucked from the Camellia sinensis plant, then quickly heated to prevent oxidation. This process gives green teas their mellow flavor, often tasting earthy, nutty, and herbaceous.

Green teas are often caffeinated, and if you're looking for a pleasant alternative to coffee that is entirely different in flavor, then you'll have luck with green teas. Green tea is consumed in many places worldwide, and it comes in many forms, from the powdered matcha to grassy sencha. In the US, you can even get small, concentrated cups of matcha tea and drink it like you would a shot of liquor. Green teas are varied and nuanced while still being one of the most consumed teas in the world.

**Tip #1: Genmaicha, a green tea flavored with roasted brown rice (that sometimes looks like popcorn!), can help with digestion issues. Genmaicha, along with many other green teas, is a strong diuretic, meaning it will help your body lose excess water and salt. It can reduce bloating, decrease indigestion, or help you feel a little more spritely, though you'll likely be thirsty later.**

With many more out there, here are a few of the most common types of green tea:

- Sencha: a commonly consumed green tea in Japan. Sencha teas typically taste faintly nutty with pleasant grassy notes.
- Matcha: one of the only teas in which you will actually drink the leaves. Matcha teas are made from powdered tea leaves. Matcha teas often taste earthy and are a great source of antioxidants and caffeine.
- Kukicha: one of the only teas made with stems and twigs rather than leaves. Kukicha teas are nutty and slightly sweet, creating a rich, yellow brew.
- Fukamushicha: Fukamushicha teas are deep-steamed, combining several other green teas to provide a bold, rich flavor. As a bonus, when brewing it yourself, some tea participles will coat the bottom of your cup, and similar to matcha, drinking those little bits of tea leaves provides health benefits.

# _Black Tea_

Black tea is the favorite of much of the Western world, with a solid seat in the UK and North America. Black teas tend to have a bold and dominating flavor, and they make for great morning teas when you need to get a running start to your day. Earl Grey is one of the best-known black teas, and its citrus tang and mellow floral notes are well known to lovers of black tea.

Black tea became popular in England after its production in British-occupied India in the 19th century. Black teas are made by letting tea leaves oxidize after being picked, allowing the flavors to deepen just as the color of the leaves grows darker. Black teas are commonly consumed as a mellow alternative to coffee, but they have their own merit that makes them more than just a substitute.

**Tip #2: If you want to wake up quickly or add some vigor to your day, black teas are often as caffeinated as coffee without the strain on your digestive system. Many types of coffee are acidic and harsh on the stomach lining, but tea is rarely so intense so that you can get all the benefits of the caffeine boost with none of the stomach trouble.**

**Tip #3: Black teas can be flavored with cream and sugar similarly to coffee while still retaining their unique flavors. Black teas have intense, bold flavors that will shine through even strong flavor additives like cream, so**

**don't be afraid to mix it up and give yourself something delicious.**

**Tip #4: If the flavor of a Masala Chai is not to your liking, you can alter the blend yourself by adding spices directly to your cup to embolden the flavor or milk to soften it. Try adding a dash of nutmeg and a tiny sprinkle of cayenne for some extra kick. If you want something flavorful to cut through the sweetness but don't want spice, cinnamon is also a common spice for a good Chai.**

Below is a small sampling of common black teas:

- Darjeeling: Named after the Darjeeling District in India, where the British originally began growing and exporting their tea, Darjeeling black tea is often called the "champagne of teas" for its sweet and musky flavor combining notes of citrus with a subtle earthy undercurrent.
- Earl Grey: This common black tea, flavored with bergamot oil, has layers of citrus and is often supplemented with lavender, orange, or vanilla. Its distinctive smell, flavor, and reputation make it one of the most well-known black teas around the world.
- Choose your country Breakfast blends: English, Irish, and Scottish are the most common breakfast blends, and they each contain different rations of black tea blends. Commonly compared to Earl Grey, these teas typically do not have Earl Grey's characteristic bergamot

flavor and instead rely on the bold, rich flavors of blended black tea.

- Masala Chai: Bold black tea is mixed with aromatic Indian herbs and spices to create an often-spicy tea that can be combined with milk or cream. Masala Chai teas vary in flavor and spice depending on where they are mixed, with some being sweet and milky and others being spicy and challenging.

## *White Tea*

Many of the most gentle teas are white teas. Their flavors are soft and floral, and the leaves themselves are often a pale green. Often accented with lavender and honey, white teas can range from fruity to bold and nutty. White teas are also known for their enchanting aromas, many of which are enticing enough before the tea has even been brewed.

Where black tea is plucked and then left to oxidize, white tea is carefully treated to keep oxidation to an absolute minimum, which gives these teas their characteristic subtle flavors. White tea is often floral in taste, soothing, gentle, and as delicate as the budding leaves from which it is made.

**Tip #5: Some white teas, like Jasmine Pearl tea, will bloom when you steep them, so grab a transparent cup and watch your tea come back to life. Pearl teas will open and wave their long leaves. Other blooming teas even have flowers in them that will open for a beautiful view.**

Here is a small list of white teas to entice you to search for more:

- Jasmine: With a floral, summery flavor, Jasmine tea has one of the most recognizable scents of any tea. With subtle caffeine and a strong flavor, Jasmine tea is as distinctive as it is delicious.
- Silver Needle: Silver Needle teas, made from thin, dried white tea leaves, are smooth and gentle in their flavor, often carrying hints of citrus.
- White Peony: Mild yet fruity, these teas are among the bolder brews white tea has to offer. Reminiscent of green tea, White Peony tea is sweet and sometimes nutty.
- Long Life Eyebrow tea: Stronger than Silver Needle or even White Peony, Long Life Eyebrow tea, often called longevity tea, is defined by a bold yet quenching flavor.

## *Oolong Tea*

Oolong teas are rare in many parts of the world, but that rarity makes them that much more of a goal for tea drinkers. Wildly variable, it is said there is an Oolong tea for everyone. If you want a robust tea tasting of fruit and loam or if you want a complex floral flavor that falls across your tongue, either way, there's an Oolong for that.

Oxidized for longer than Green Tea but shorter than Black Tea, Oolong tea is a strongly flavored middle ground. Containing deeper notes of the nutty flavors that characterize green teas along with the subtle richness of black teas, Oolong is often complex in flavor and deeply satisfying.

**Tip #6: Though hard to find in many places, Oolong teas are often the answer when you want a little caffeine but mostly want something delicious. Oolong teas are complex and diverse, so if you have a specific flavor you want, whether it's smoky and strong or sweet and soft, there's likely an Oolong for you.**

Below is a sample of Oolong teas, but there are many more, each complex and unique:

- Red Robe: The warm brown color of this tea matches the complex roasted flavor it provides. While it contains some of the depth of black tea, Red Robe also carries notes of citrus.
- Phoenix: In contrast to Red Robe, Phoenix Oolong tea is naturally fruity, often supplemented with honey to coax the sweet flavors even further.
- Iron Goddess: Combining the vegetal taste of green tea with the fruity offerings of Phoenix Oolong, Iron Goddess is a complex tea that is fresh and invigorating.
- Milk: Floral yet smooth, sweet yet buttery, Milk Oolong is refreshing, soothing, and gentle on the throat.

# *Herbal Tea*

While herbal tea has origins in different plants, it is no less a valued member of the tea family. With documented medicinal benefits, many herbal teas have been consumed for thousands of years. Home remedies and orders from the doctor alike account for herbal teas. If something ails you, the odds are good there is a delicate blend of herbs that can help soothe you.

Herbal tea, technically speaking, is not tea. Tea comes from the leaves of the Camellia sinensis, and herbal tea does not contain those leaves, but tea has evolved beyond the confines of one leaf, and herbal teas are as entrenched in tea culture like any other. Semantics are subservient to pleasure, and herbal teas are joyful and delicious. Flavored by the herbs they're named after, Herbal teas are medicinal, gentle, often fruity, and each one is distinct.

**Tip #7: Throat coat, a familiar blend of licorice, Elm, and Marshmallow root, can be a great tea before bed if you had a day full of talking or if you're noticing a tickle in your throat. The blend of herbs will do exactly as the name of the tea suggests, coating your throat in a soothing layer of gentle, healing herbs.**

**Tip #8: Mint tea can help with indigestion, and if you add a little sugar, it tastes like mint candy. Peppermint, the main and often only ingredient in mint tea, can help to relax your stomach, easing indigestion and bloating. Animals have been seen in the wild eating it for this exact reason.**

**Tip #9:** If you are looking for a calm tea to close out your day, herbal teas are rarely caffeinated, and the gentle flavors will lull you to a pleasant, healthy slumber. With delicate flavors and soothing health benefits, many herbal teas are perfect for when you want to take your time falling into a quiet, easy sleep.

Here are several of the most commonly consumed herbal teas, but they are as diverse as the herbs from which they are derived:

- Chamomile: Looking like daisies and tasting like floral sleep, Chamomile has long been a soothing remedy that can be supplemented with honey, vanilla, or lemon.
- Peppermint: Peppermint tea, made from dried mint leaves, has a robust and nourishing flavor of earthy mint.
- Ginger: Spicy and wholesome like the root it comes from, Ginger tea is a zesty delight that is often blended with Green teas.
- Rose: Made from rose hips, rose tea is subtle, pink, and gentle. Flourishing when mixed with honey, these teas are floral, tart, and sweet.

## *Chapter Review*

- Tea is a beverage as diverse as the people who love it.
- Enjoyed around the world, tea has developed from the leaves of a single plant into a wide variety of drinks.

- Tea can largely be broken down into a few distinct families: Green, Black, White, Oolong, and Herbal.
- Green teas are nutty, grassy, and richly flavored.
- Black teas are highly caffeinated, bold, and the closest in flavor to coffee.
- White teas are delicate, fruity, and sweet.
- Oolong teas are complex, offer a range of flavors bordering the boldness of black teas and the nuttiness of green tea.
- Herbal teas are not made from the same plant all other teas come from; rather, they are made from herbs themselves and are flavored as differently as the herbs they're named after.

# Chapter 2: Bags, Sachets, and Loose Leaf

## *Tea Delivery Methods*

Making tea is, overall, a pretty simple act. Generally, it follows a very intuitive formula in which dry leaves plus hot water equals some tasty beverage. However, certain leaves will decide the flavor, how long it rests in the water, what you'll add to it, and a myriad of other things. And beyond just choosing which leaves, you also get to decide how exactly you want to present those leaves to their hot water final destination.

Overall, there are three main ways of getting your tea into a nice pot of hot water: bags, sachets, and infusers. Bags and sachets generally have relatively fine leaves, sometimes ground nearly to a powder, and infusers are used for loose leaf tea.

When we think about the different kinds of tea delivery systems, we can also think about grocery shopping. The two are natural parallels. When I go to the store, I generally try to bring my own shopping bags. I have a few of the canvas bags, the ones that aren't that sturdy but are much bigger than the plastic bags I'd have to deal with if I didn't bring my own. I find that when I bring a bigger bag with me, my groceries tend to fare a bit better than if they were all packed together in a plastic bag. Legions of avocados owe their unbruised bodies to my delightful shopping bags.

When I forget my bags at home, stuffed under the sink inside a yet larger bag, I either have to use plastic bags or, as I like to do, I leave everything in the cart-no bags, living dangerously, all my fresh produce mingling in the big steel cage of the cart.

This riveting discussion of grocery delivery methods is a perfect parallel for the three types of containers you'll use for tea: bags, sachets, and infusers.

## *Bags*

Nearly everyone has seen a teabag. You'll find them in almost any grocery store and see their labels dangling from cups and travel mugs in office buildings and classrooms. I used to even keep a bag of English Breakfast with me at all times, just for emergencies.

Teabags are common because they're easy to use and brew quickly. You can go from having a wimpy pot of bland hot water to a robust, beautiful tea in a few short minutes if you have a teabag on hand.

Teabags tend to pack their tea in tight. If you take a look at the contents of many teabags, you won't even find a recognizable leaf. Instead, you'll find a powder. The reason for both the ground tea is that it will diffuse in your water quicker. It's uniform in size and shape, so you don't have to worry about any of the flavors not getting exposure to the water. However, in the name of speed, many tea brands also overfill their bags. You get what is essentially two or three cups worth of tea packed into one bag, so of course, it will steep faster and give a more robust flavor.

**Tip #10: Tea bags are great for traveling with tea. They're portable, brew quickly, and the flavor is generally very strong, which can be nice when you're drinking tea on the go.**

**Tip #11: Do not open a teabag. They're often sealed with heat or tied tightly to close them. If you open your bag, there's no guarantee you can get that same seal, and you'll likely end up with a gritty cup full of fine tea grounds.**

**Tip #12: If you're using a tea bag in a travel mug, leave a little space without water so you can pull the bag up to stop it from over-steeping. It is great for when you're in a hurry and don't have a moment to remove your bag.**

## _Sachets_

Sachets are less common than tea bags, but that doesn't make them hard to find. Our second tea container is the sachet, which is basically just a nice tea bag. These bags are bigger, generally contain higher quality tea, and only rarely grind their tea to the same fine powder you'd see in a teabag. In tea sachets, you can generally find whole leaf tea, and the extra room for expansion means the tea can expand without blocking any other flavors from the water. Tea sachets are often a good indicator that a brand is a little higher quality, if for no reason other than that you can see the tea inside them so they can't get away with overfilling.

**Tip #13: Be careful using tea sachets. Many of them use a tiny piece of wax or glue to affix the label and string before you unravel it, and if you're not careful, you can rip the sachet and spill tea everywhere.**

## *Infusers*

Our final delivery method is an infuser, and these are generally only used for loose leaf tea, though sometimes I like to throw an orange peel in one to add some flavor to a bland cup. Loose leaf tea is a tea that does not come packaged in bags or sachets. It's left to you to portion it out, and either fill bags of your own or use an infuser to make the perfect cup.

The first time I bought my own loose leaf tea, I had no idea what to do with it. It was a beautiful earl grey that came in a tiny glass jar with a cork, and I felt like an apothecary taking it home. Before I got home, I put it in my pocket and immediately forgot about it, and there it stayed for a few days until a visitor arrived. I didn't have many visitors, and this one happened to come at the crack of noon when I was waking up. I woke up to a firm knocking on my door, saw through my window that it was one of my teachers that had somehow found my tiny, rundown apartment and was at my door. I panicked, tried to make myself look presentable, and just before I got to the door, I realized my breath was probably pretty disagreeable. I patted my pockets for some gum and instead found a jar that I remembered contained delicious smelling tea. I popped the cork, shoved the tea in my mouth, and hoped for the best when I answered the door. That was the wrong way to use loose leaf tea.

**Tip #14: Do not eat your loose leaf tea. I cannot imagine any logical reason to do this. It is very unpleasant, and any onlookers can tell you've just shoved a handful of tea into your mouth.**

What I should have done was this:

1. Go home without forgetting my jar of tea in my pocket.
2. Put on the kettle at a temperature appropriate for black tea.
3. Sprinkle my delicious prize into an infuser (I also should have bought one of those) and brew myself a lovely cup of my favorite tea in the world. While drinking it, I should have also checked my email to find that one of my profcssors, who also happened to be my boss, really wanted to talk to me.

**Tip #15: Use an infuser to brew your loose leaf teas. Infusers come in a million shapes and sizes, but their shared purpose is to contain your tea in a sort of cage that gives it ample room for expansion and submersion.**

**Tip #16:** You can find and buy infusers at almost any dedicated tea shop. If you don't see them there, you can find many online.

**Tip #17:** When you get an infuser, find one with a fine mesh or tiny holes. You want your tea exposed to water, but you also don't want your tea getting into that water. If you have rogue leaves drifting around your cup, they'll continue to steep and make your drink bitter.

## *When Do You Want Loose Leaf vs. Bags and Sachets*

There is no wrong type of tea if you enjoy it. If you like the taste of tea you get in a bag, then keep brewing it. If you prefer the tea you tend to find in a sachet, get that, and the same goes for loose leaf. However, if you tend to like all three, there are specific times when a bag may be better for your beverage than a sachet or loose leaf tea.

The strengths of a teabag are in its portability and the intensity of the brew. While the tea may not always be of the best quality and can go bitter faster, there are undoubtedly times when a tea bag is the most sensible thing for the intrepid tea drinker.

Teabags are great for when you want a cup of tea quickly or when you're going to be drinking tea on the go. If you're at home, tired, maybe at the end of a late-night or the start of an early morning, you probably won't want to fiddle around with the different moving parts to make a good cup of loose leaf tea. You also may not want to dig into your nicer tea because you're in it a bit for taste but primarily for utility. If you need to wake up, bagged tea works as well as any other kind, often better because there's just more tea packed into the bag.

I consider sachets the middle ground of tea. They aren't nearly as involved as loose leaf brews, but they also are usually a little more delicate than tea bags. Because of that, a sachet is suitable for when you want some good quality tea, but you also don't want to put that much effort into it. Sachets are already measured out to the perfect size you need for a cup and are usually flavorful and delicious. If you want a good cup of tea but don't really have it in you to go through all the steps to make that happen, a sachet is where you want to go. I would also recommend this as a prime lunch-tea because you have the mental capacity to put a bit more thought into it, but it doesn't take so much time that it will distract from more pressing endeavors, like sandwiches.

Loose-leaf teas are perfect for when you want a delicious cup of tea, and you're in a place where you can enjoy every step it takes to make that happen. Because loose-leaf brews are a bit more involved, often it takes a dedicated few minutes to make it right between measuring out the right amount, picking the infuser you want to use, deciding if you're going to mix anything into the blend, etc. There's so much you can customize at every stage of your loose leaf brew, and that lends itself to making it during a time when you can sit down and make those decisions. For that reason, I tend to brew loose leaf tea when I have a free hour and want to dedicate about a third of it to brewing tea and the rest to enjoying it.

The thing to take away from this chapter is not that there is a right kind of tea or that there is a right time to make it. Understanding tea is the best way to ensure you get the best experience possible. Knowing the strengths of each type of tea is worthwhile because it can give you the information you need to make yourself the best brew specifically for you.

If you love your bagged tea dearly for all occasions, keep going with it. I still cling to my beloved Twining's Earl Grey every morning, and I won't give it up even though I have a jar of delicious loose leaf Earl Grey right next to it. Stick with what you like, but learn what it is about it that you like so you can replicate it in other brews. If you enjoy a strong cup of tea but want to branch out into sachets or loose-leaf, you can always add another sachet of tea to your cup or add another spoon of tea to your infuser. If you like seeing the leaves twirl and spin in an expanding sachet, there are glass pots of tea specifically designed for replicating that with loose leaf tea. There are even blooming teas with flowers and petals in them specifically because they look as pretty as they taste. And if you like loose leaf tea, not just because you can customize it endlessly, but because you enjoy the ceremony and steps to make it, you can still replicate that with other teas. Get a fancy spoon for your honey, or start taking your sugar in cube form with cute little tongs, whatever works for you.

# *Chapter Review*

- There are three main delivery methods for tea: bags, sachets, and infusers
- Bags are densely packed and often contain ground tea
- But bags also brew quickly and leave a strong flavor, though that also means they can go bitter fast
- Sachets are delicate bags of tea that are larger and often contain full leaves of the tea
- Sachets expand to fully immerse every part of the tea in water so it can diffuse effectively
- Sachets are often a sign of a slightly higher quality brand, but they are also rather delicate. If you're too rough with a sachet, it may break and fill your cup with delicious, beautiful, quickly bittering leaves of the tea
- Infusers are used for loose leaf tea
- Loose-leaf teas are teas that have not been packaged for you. They are more customizable and blendable, but you also have to measure them yourself
- Infusers are containers for loose leaf tea, often metal, with holes or a grate that allows water to flow freely through the tea without letting any tea leaves escape into the water. A good infuser will be large enough for the tea to expand
- There is no one perfect type of tea. Each delivery method is useful for different purposes, and it's up to you to decide what you enjoy most.

# Chapter 3: What You'll Need

## *My First Tea Cup*

When I first fell in love with tea, beyond enjoying it as a not-coffee beverage or thinking of it as an infrequent novelty, I was drinking it out of a $5 cup I'd bought from Target that also doubled as my only bowl. That cup spent its life cooking 10 cent instant noodles and delivering an unwholesome amount of coffee to my body. I had been watching a lot of Star Trek: The Next Generation and had gotten intrigued by a line that Captain Picard repeated at least once, seemingly every episode. "Earl Grey. Hot."

So I bought some Bigelow Earl Grey, poured some water into my only cup, put that cup into the microwave, then I waited. While the water heated, maybe I had fantasized about going to some popular coffee shop and getting to try out Picard's line for my own. Still, that fantasy was as self-indulgent as it was for me to break out one of my only remaining sugar packets for this drink I didn't even think I'd like. I remember smelling the bag of tea dangling in my hands, like citrus and hotel rooms. A few minutes later, I was back at my desk, chaotically covered in discarded papers and empty cans that once held energy drinks. I sat down, the tea having steeped already, and plopped a dot of French vanilla cream into my cup and swirled it with the back of a pen. I emptied half of my sugar packet into it, watched a faint tan foam bloom from the bottom. I took one sip, said to an empty room likely after midnight, "Ooh that's decadent," and that was it for me.

After that, I was tea-obsessed. All of my travel mugs of coffee got a thorough washing, then a second thorough washing, then a generous scraping to get rid of the patina of coffee that had coated them. They would never again be touched by anything but tea, usually Earl Grey. I found that drinking tea had the same waking influence on me, but I didn't feel ragged and worn out after it had worn off. Tea was a gentle but forceful hand in my life, carrying me through the latter days of my time in college. I traded my coffee maker for a cheap electric kettle. It was mostly plastic, and by the time I was done with it, the spout had warped from the near-constant use. I liked my Earl Grey hot.

I make tea a little differently now, and I use it for a different purpose. Tea can be a strong drink, and like coffee, it can be used as a pick-me-up throughout the day, but I found that I enjoyed it more if I was drinking tea for the tea and not for its effects on my body. If I want an Earl Grey now, I'll have one, and if it wakes me up in the morning, that's lovely, but I try not to need that. For me, tea is something to be enjoyed, not prescribed.

When I make my tea now, I use an electric kettle with multiple temperature settings instead of a cup in a microwave. Instead of stirring my tea with the back of a pen or a chopstick that lost its sibling, I have a few specially sized spoons perfect for scooping honey. Instead of pre-bagged Earl Grey, I tend to drink loose leaf or bag my own. I even print off my own label and brewing instructions. I'll be the first to admit it's adorable, and I do it entirely because of the satisfaction I get seeing my name in cursive next to a blend of tea I've prepared.

A lot has changed, but my way of drinking tea before wasn't wrong, just like my way of drinking it now isn't necessarily correct. Tea is a drink. The only way you can drink a drink wrong is if you don't drink it at all. I do that a lot too, and the constant supply of cold cups around my home is evidence of that. There are different methods and apparatus for making tea, and many of these methods have been shared and perfected across generations for as long as there have been tea, and sometimes those methods make the tea taste really good, and that's nice too.

If you are looking to make the best tea, the first thing you need to consider is how you're making it, specifically, what tools are you using? I loved my microwave tea, and the cup I used to boil water was my very favorite cup, but once I started diversifying my tea-making tools, I noticed I liked the taste even more, and maybe that first cup was good despite being brewed in the same cup I used to make soup.

You won't always use all of them, but there are four main categories for the tools you'll need to brew your tea.

- Water heater
- Place to brew
- Infuser or Bag tray
- Something to drink from

# _Water Heaters_

In my time making and drinking tea, I've made many mistakes and seen some styles of brewing that left me wondering if we were making the same drink. The most common error I made was microwaving my water or microwaving my water and my tea in some cases. One of the worst cups of tea I've made myself was because, while half asleep, I threw a tea bag into a cup, poured cold water over it, then tossed the whole thing in a microwave. I learned two things that night.

1) Microwaved tea doesn't taste quite right.
2) Many tea bags are stapled closed.

So after buying a new microwave, I vowed not to microwave my tea anymore, if only because the image of my little white teacup illuminated by brilliant white flashes of light and fire wasn't something I wanted to see twice.

The most baffling way I've seen tea made was without any actual heating apparatus. It wasn't iced tea or sun tea, both delicious and to be discussed later. It was a college freshman turning the faucet to hot, filling a cup, and plopping a bag of Moroccan mint into it. I didn't say anything at the time, but I tried it myself later that night. It tasted exactly like I expected, like weak tea in lukewarm water from a dorm room sink. I don't fault anyone for how they enjoy their tea, but I have to wonder if he was really enjoying it at all.

I don't microwave my tea water anymore, and that's because microwaves do not heat water evenly. When you microwave a cup of water, what you're left with is a cup of water in which some is boiling, some are near-boiling, and some is something else entirely. Tea likes consistent temperature, so you don't want tiny pockets of warm, cool, and hot water giving your tea an inconsistent brew. To get the most flavor out of your tea, you **need to brew it at the right temperature, so that's where a kettle comes in.**

**Tip #18: Tea kettles are the best way to heat your water because they're temperature controlled. Kettles will boil water to the same temperature every time, and some even have different temperatures for different kinds of teas already built-in!**

**Tip #19: If you find yourself making only one type of tea, you can get a kettle that only goes up to the temperature you need it at. Those tend to be a bit cheaper too!**

Picking the proper kettle for you requires an understanding of the kind of tea you like to make. If you're making many different kinds of tea, bouncing between green and black and Oolong and white, then you'll want a kettle that can brew to the different temperatures suited to your various teas. White and Oolong teas tend to brew at a lower temperature, often anywhere from 170 - 190 degrees Fahrenheit. Black and herbal teas tend to go for hotter temperatures, usually between 205 and 215 degrees Fahrenheit. Finding a kettle that can consistently meet those temperatures when you want them is essential to getting the right flavor out of your tea. If you go too cool for black tea, the taste will not come out. If you go too hot for white teas, the delicate flavors will grow bitter in the intense heat.

**Tip #20: While you're shopping for a kettle, check how the cord will rest below the kettle. Many have a convenient little nook cut out so the cable won't destabilize your kettle, but some don't, and you want to avoid any device that permanently has boiling water nearly tipping over.**

## *A Place to Brew*

I got my first teapot about two weeks after that decadent cup of Earl Grey. I didn't even know what teapots were for. I just knew I wanted one, and the one I found was a rich reddish-brown and could hold three full cups of tea within it.

I always had a fascination with teapots. Maybe it was their elephantine shape or the million designs you can find, but I've loved them since long before I loved tea, and that first teapot cemented my love. The proper teapot can be a place to brew your tea, keep it warm, and give yourself a little aesthetic flavor to boot.

**Tip #21: If you're shopping for a teapot, pay special attention to size and material. A glass teapot, while beautiful, will not keep your tea warm for as long as a clay one.**

**Tip #22:** If you are using a metal teapot or kettle, be careful of the lid. It shouldn't be surprising that metal can get hot, but when you're distracted by imminent tea, mistakes happen. If you love the look of a metal teapot, look for one with wooden or plastic handles that will not retain heat as cruelly.

**Tip #23:** Make sure there are no plastic parts on your teapot if you're planning on using it for a long time. Plastic can warp and crumble, and nobody wants flecks of plastic in their Darjeeling.

A teapot is a diverse tool. You can brew your tea in it; often, they even come with a built-in infuser for loose leaf tea. If you're using bagged tea, most teapots are big enough to accommodate several cups of tea, so you can comfortably use several bags. Beyond just being a place to brew, teapots also keep your tea fresh and hot. Most good teapots will keep your tea warm for a little while.

**Tip #24:** If you plan on having long gaps between cups of tea, find a tea light you can place your teapot on top of. The candle or electric heater will keep your brew warmer for longer.

## *Infuser or Bag Tray*

The first time I bought a tea infuser, I had no idea what it was. All I knew was the teashop behind my apartment had a golden ball with star-shaped holes all over it for sale, and I wanted it whether I knew what it did or not. I remember setting aside my impulse purchase for a long time until I started drinking loose leaf tea. Once I tried using my beautiful little infuser to make tea, I found that it was as beautiful as it was terrible at its job. As beautiful as my golden ball full of stars was, it really wasn't suitable for much more than appearances.

Opening the thing was infuriating as it used a tiny latch that rusted shut instead of clicking closed like most infusers. The holes to let the water and tea mingle were far too big. As pretty as it was to see beautiful, infused tea water pouring from star holes, it was less appealing to see a million flecks of tea leaves also floating into my cup. Drinking from a cup brewed with that infuser was like ripping open a tea bag and brewing its contents directly in my mouth.

When they work, tea infusers are incredibly useful for loose leaf tea. They come in all manner of shapes and sizes, but they all do the same thing: contain your loose leaf tea so it can steep without filling your water with hundreds of tiny leaves. Infusers are essentially reusable tea bags that you can fill with the loose leaf tea of your choice. A good tea infuser will contain your leaves while letting enough water move through it to allow the tea to infuse the water around it fully.

Often infusers are flawed in the same ways: they don't have enough space beneath the water for the tea, particularly true among the infusers that hang from the side of your cup. Or they will have too wide of openings like my beautiful one did, and you'll find your water both thoroughly infused and completely blanketed with tea leaves.

Finding a suitable infuser can mean having easy access to a much wider variety of delicious teas. It can be a pain to brew for all the various loose leaf tea offers because you need to either bag it yourself or find a reliable infuser.

**Tip #25: If you find you have to chew your delicious tea beverage, find an infuser with smaller openings. You don't want much or any loose leaf tea remaining in your cup when you're done brewing, and it has an awful texture on the teeth.**

If you are using tea bags, then you have likely encountered the conundrum of finding somewhere to put them that doesn't require leaving your beverage to carry a sopping used tea bag toward a trash can. Most tea bags are filled enough that they'll brew quickly and leave you with a strong flavor, so leaving the bag in your cup or pot isn't an option.

What's left to you is to find a bag tray, a little plate that doesn't take up too much room but can hold your tea bags until you're through with them. Finding the right place to put your used tea bag can be as important as keeping your tea warm or finding the right infuser. It's all part of a good tea experience, and finding a tray that doesn't deposit the dregs onto your desk is an essential part of a good tea time.

**Tip #26: Find a bag tray with raised edges so you won't spill the dregs everywhere. You**

don't want to stain your clothes or furniture just because you didn't want your tea to get bitter.


## *Something to Drink From*

Needing a cup to drink from may seem like it's not worth stating, but finding the right cup is what you're really trying to do. A cup of the right material is as crucial to enjoying your tea as finding the proper teapot to brew it and keep it warm. The wrong cup can let your tea get cool too fast, spoil the flavor, or even be dangerous.

Ceramic cups and mugs are great all-purpose teacups. They're sturdy, retain their heat well, come in a million shapes and designs, and are generally heat resistant. Tea is a hot beverage, so don't forget that you can burn yourself on the cup as easily as with the drink itself.

The only wrong cup for drinking tea is one that doesn't keep your drink warm and your eyes happy. With so much variety in teacups, find one that fits your mood and enjoy it.

**Tip #27: If you find your tea is growing cold too quickly in your cup, consider pouring less and keeping the rest in a temperature-controlled container like a pot or thermos. Small cups mean you can drink them quickly and keep your tea at that perfect temperature.**

**Tip #28: Brightly colored teacups look pretty and are a bit harder to forget. One of the most common ways a cup of tea is wasted is by setting it aside to cool and only remembering it once it's cold.**

**Tip #29: Though they are a novel concept, most electric mug warmers are not strong enough to keep your tea at an optimal temperature. Keep track of your tea and drink it when it's ready.**

Materials to avoid

- Plastic: repeated exposure to boiling water can warp it, and it will often leave your tea with a synthetic, plastic flavor.
- Disposable plastic: this bears emphasis because many disposable cups are very thin plastic, and the boiling water or tea will not do well in them. The thin plastic is also terrible for heat retention, meaning you'll burn your hands, and your tea will get cold, the worst of both worlds.
- Untempered glass: Many teacups are glass. They let you look at the beautiful colors of your brew, see pearls of tea opening and flowers blooming. They're lovely, and they're specifically built to hold high-temperature liquids. Untempered glass is not designed to go from room temperature to 200 degrees Fahrenheit in a matter of seconds, and there is nothing that can ruin a cup of tea like shards of glass from an exploding cup. Tempered glass is made to withstand high temperatures, and it

retains heat much better, so your tea will last longer.

## *Other Useful Tea Tools*

**Tea Spoons:** if you're a user of loose leaf tea, find a small spoon you can use any time you want to scoop your tea, whether it's into a bag, an infuser, or a pot. Standardizing how much tea you get per scoop can help you predict the strength of your brew. As a bonus, you can find many spoons designed for this exact purpose that are absolutely beautiful. I have one that looks like a rose, and I love it.

**Honey dispenser:** if you love honey in your tea, then a good dispenser is invaluable. With the right one, you won't have to worry about sticky spoons or frozen jar lids ever again, and they look beautiful with your tea set. You can find ones that you can hold over your cup or pot and release a single stream of honey from the bottom, or you can go the traditional route and find a nice jar with a honey wand.

**Tea organizer:** if you have a hundred different kinds of tea, getting a box or shelf to organize your teas can make it much easier to see everything you have. You can find many beautiful wooden tea boxes for cheap, and they'll make picking out a tea less a scramble for the flavor you know you have and more of a gentle shopping trip in your own home.

# *Chapter Review*

- The apparatus to brew tea is as necessary as the tea itself.
- At a baseline, you need only four things: a way to heat water, a place for your tea to steep, a way to steep it, and something to drink out of.
- Beyond the basics, catering to the brewing requirements of each tea is essential, and there are various tools to ensure you can easily do that.

# Chapter 4: What to add

## *Never Too Much Honey*

I am a firm believer that there has never been too much honey added to a cup of tea. I like my chamomile gold and my English breakfast to taste like a beehive, but getting to that point required a lot of experimentation. My first cup of Earl Grey as an adult had milk and sugar, and I just accidentally happened upon the perfect ratio to make a cup so enticing that I never stopped wanting more. Shortly after I finished that first cup, I tried to make another.

I seemingly added the same amount of sugar and milk, and the tea was good, but it wasn't perfect. It wasn't that flawless tincture that got me to sing its praises to a totally empty room. I started experimenting more with the ratios of milk to sugar, then I changed things up and just added whatever sounded good. Herbal tea? Throw some lemon in there. Black tea? Toss in some lavender. I played it fast and loose with herbal supplements for a time before I fell in love with honey. White tea? Give it some honey? Green tea, also honey. Add honey.

Eventually, I arrived at a series of general conclusions that helped me make my tea how I liked it, and I've found that others have reached similar conclusions.

**Tip #30: Natural ingredients work well to flavor tea. Avoid synthetic flavors because**

they tend to 1) overpower the subtle flavors of
the tea and 2) lack some of the health benefits
natural ingredients contain.

**Tip #31: Less is more when it comes to adding
things to your cup. Where it might take a lot of
cream to stand out in your coffee, just a little
can have the same effect on a cup of tea. Start
off adding small portions until you find the
flavor that suits you.**

For organization, we can break down the types of
additives one might use for modifying tea. These
categories may not encompass everything one might
use to enhance their brew, but it captures the
significant components.

## *Creams*

Variants of milk, whether it comes from an animal, a
plant, or science, fall under this category. Many use
creams to soften the flavor of a tea. Bitter teas can
have their taste lightened with the right cream, and
teas with overpowering flavors can become
comfortably muted.

Which cream you use is entirely dependent on
personal preference and dietary needs because the
overlap in flavors and textures is significant. While the
taste of oat milk and dairy milk might be considerably
disparate when drinking them plain, once they have
been mixed into a tea, it takes some extra attention or
a very discerning taste to discern the difference.

**Tip #32: Add cream sparingly. A little goes a long way, and once you have added it, the only way to bring the tea flavor back is to add more already-brewed tea.**

**Tip #33: You don't have to settle for simply adding cream to your tea. Most tea shops will make you a tea latte with the cream of your choice. Varying how you consume tea is a wonderful way to keep it fresh.**

## *Sweeteners*

Sweeteners often fill the same role as creams without altering the flavor and texture of the tea significantly. A little bit of sweetness can cut through the bitter taste of most teas, even ones that have been slightly over-steeped. Picking the right sweeteners is also dependent on your personal flavor preferences, but it is also important to avoid making your tea into a syrup.

Some of the most common sweeteners you'll encounter are sugar and honey, with synthetic sweeteners following close behind. Though less prominent than creams, sweeteners do bring their own flavor to your tea. Aspartame may sweeten your cup while also leaving a slightly synthetic taste behind. Enough sugar can leave some teas tasting of caramel. Adding significant amounts of honey will leave the tea tasting, remarkably, of honey. Use sweeteners when you want to reduce bitterness or have a bit more levity in your cup.

Tip #34: Honey has documented health benefits. It is believed that using the honey from local bees can even improve your resistance to pollen-based allergies, and it supports local beekeepers! Honey is not magic, but it certainly tastes like it!

Tip #35: Some medicinal teas like throat coat contain licorice or other flavors that are not universally enjoyed. Adding a spoonful of sugar can always help the medicine go down.

Tip #36: Along with the flavor and health benefits, a little honey can add an enticing golden hue to many teas, perfect if you want your drink to look as delicious as it tastes.

Tip #37: If you are mixing sweetener or any kind of added flavor with your tea, and you find you've added too much, there's nothing wrong with making a new cup of tea. Tea is made to be enjoyed, so you shouldn't feel the need to power your way through a syrupy mint or an over-zesty breakfast tea. Make a new cup and try again. We only get better through practice, and failure is a great teacher.

## _Citrus_

Among the sugar packets and stirrings rods, you may have seen little yellow containers of lemon juice the last time you were at a coffee shop. A little burst of citrus can liven up your tea, pierce even the densest brews, and bring a little vitamin C into your day.

Before balking at the idea of squeezing a lemon into your morning cup, consider that Earl Grey is one of the best-known black teas, and it is beloved for its overt citrus flavor. A little spritz of lemon in your black or green tea can add a new delicious layer to your brew, highlighting existing flavors and waking your palate up.

**Tip #38: If the juice of a lemon is too strong or sour, try adding a little piece of the peel. You can do the same thing with an orange. Let it soak in your tea for a moment and experience a more muted note of citrus than if you had added the raw juice.**

**Tip #39: Be sparing with your citrus. Though it's delicious, you're still squirting lemon juice into your cup, so add a little and do a taste test. It is also recommended to drip the liquid into your cup as lemon juice is rather acidic and has been known to be unpleasant when eyes are directly exposed to it.**

**Tip #40: Many grocery stores and tea supply stores sell dried citrus peel that you can add to your tea blends on your own. If you are using loose leaf, toss a few tiny pieces of lemon peel in with your leaves and experience the same boosted flavor as adding the juice directly to it. Experiment with ratios before adding any dried ingredients to your loose leaf stockpiles. What looks like a little bit of lemon sometimes**

**ends up being much more potent than you intended.**


## *Auxiliary Flavors*

Spices, flavored syrups, other beverages, anything you might add to a tea with its own flavor could fall under this category. Many lovers of masala chai add a dusting of nutmeg and cinnamon to the top of their cup, and some who like their brew spicy also add a healthy dash of cayenne. Many made-to-order tea drinks use flavored syrups to add caramel or hazelnut or any variety of flavors to their teas, and these too fall under this category.

As with every other additive described, use all auxiliary flavors sparingly and do taste tests as you go. Where different flavors can mix and mingle with tea to an interesting effect, the danger present in some of the flavors described above is that they will become the only flavor.

**Tip #41: Use spices sparingly. They will sink and mingle with the rest of your tea, and if you add too much nutmeg to the top of your mug, odds are there's too much nutmeg in the rest of it too.**

**Tip #42: Flavor syrups like those present at large cafe chains can be purchased for your use. Mix and match and make the drinks you would have ordered for a fraction of the price.**

**Tip #43: Black teas have the most robust flavors and can absorb the most extra flavoring while still retaining their own, but they still have a limit, and at some point, you're just drinking chai-flavored caramel instead of a caramel chai.**

**Tip #44: If you find a set of spices you consistently enjoy with a blend of tea, add them to your loose lead supply. The spices can blend easily with the dried tea, and you'll have a delicious beverage ready as soon as you steep it.**

## *Chapter Review*

- Tea is already an exciting beverage, and you can expand its flavor by adding different types of delicious things after brewing.
- There's a considerable amount of things you can add to tea, but overall they can generally be categorized as creams, sweeteners, citrus, and extra flavors.
- Add as much or as little to your drink as you please, but be careful because too much can drown out the flavors of your tea.

# Chapter 5: Blended Brews

## *Lemon and Lavender*

One of my favorite teas is a lavender Earl Grey I picked up from a local tea shop. The flavors weren't complicated, but they mingled perfectly. The citrus and depth of the bergamot with the light, fragrant lavender blended to make an extraordinary drink. It was the kind of tea I liked to sit outside with and feel for a second like things were going to be ok.

One day, while on a routine grocery trip, I found a jar of lavender. On the label, it specifically said it could be mixed into your favorite teas. I had so many favorite teas that demanded a touch of lavender, so naturally, I grabbed it. On the same shelf, I also found some dried lemon peel of the same brand. Who doesn't love a touch of citrus in their tea? I was ecstatic.

I went home, eager to mix myself some of my own lavender Earl Grey. I love buying from local tea shops, but they're expensive, and I was a poor grad student at the time, so this was all very exciting.

There were a lot of things I wish I'd done-measuring, being most of them. I decided I'd make my first cup special, not just lavender but lemon too. Lemon and lavender are complementary flavors on their own, so naturally, they would beautifully accentuate the loose leaf Earl Grey I was going to blend them with. I took out my largest infuser, basically just a metal cup, and I poured my regular cup's worth of Earl Grey leaves.

I like strong tea, so I figured I'd have to put a fair amount of lemon and lavender to really taste them, so without really registering why this might be a bad idea, I poured the same amount of lavender as I did Earl Grey, then the same again with chunky, hard little lemon peels.

My kettle finished heating, and over the dreaded herbal concoction, I poured my water. I let it steep for a full 5 minutes. To my credit, it smelled fantastic, but that wasn't due to any good work on my part. That much lemon and lavender would smell good at a desert fish market.

I removed my saturated infuser. I remember the steam coming from a bed of purple flowers and expanded lemon peels. I also remember not being able to see a single tea leaf and thinking that might not be right. I plowed ahead with my mistake, and I took a sip.

And then I took another because that couldn't have been right. No, my first taste had been correct. It was the worst tea I'd ever made myself. It tasted like a flower soaked in cleaning fluid. If I'd replaced the water in my kettle with Lysol and bad thoughts, it would have tasted better than this awful concoction. I took another sip. I had to be sure. There wasn't even a hint of the tea I'd put in. It had all been swallowed by this herbal lemon tragedy that was steaming gleefully in my big yellow cup of mistakes.

I think I tried to drink it maybe four times. I kept thinking it just needed to settle, or perhaps it was too hot, or maybe I'd left the soap in the bottom of my cup, or something external had to happen to make this go so wrong.

Something had happened to make my tea go wrong. If I'd split it between bags, I calculated later that I'd put about 13 bags' worth of lavender into that single cup and around 20 of lemon. Lemon and lavender are both deceptively strong flavors. For lavender, you don't want to confuse mellow with subtle. Mellow is calm and even, a flavor that doesn't take precedent but is still very much there. It doesn't take a lot of lavender to have the flavor peek into a brew. And lemon... it's lemon. Lemon is a citrus fruit, a sour, loud, and emphatic flavor that can accentuate other flavors if it's used right or jump to the forefront if it's used wrong. Lemon peel is also uniquely bitter. If you need a source for proof, bite a lemon like an apple, then apologize to yourself and your dentist.

## What are Blends

There are two ways to change the flavor of a tea. You can add things while it's brewing or just after, or you can do it before the tea ever meets water. When you add items to the tea itself, to the bag, sachet, loose leaf mixture, you create your own blend. Tea gets its flavor in part from the leaf itself, a part from flavor and heat treatments, and part from what it is brewed with. You can easily make your own blend by adding things to your tea before you brew it.

**Tip #45: If you're making a blend, you will usually want to do this with loose leaf tea. If you try it with a tea bag or sachet, there's a good chance you won't be able to seal them back up, and you'll end up with a cup full of tea grounds. Making a blend with loose leaf tea also means you can make a lot of it without too much added effort, rather than opening and closing dozens of individual bags.**

By mixing and matching new flavors, you can make endless delicious permutations of tea, catering specifically to your tastes and preferences. If you find that you like the flavor of a tea but wish it had more depth, you can add an herbaceous background to your tea. If you enjoy seasonally themed beverages, you can make a blend with your favorite seasonal flavors. One of the teas I most look forward to is a local shop's Autumn apple chai, which adds cinnamon sticks and dried apple to a chai to make it taste more like fall.

Making your own tea blends opens nearly endless doors for what you can do, but for simplicity's sake, we can boil down our options to 4 main flavors you can add to your teas: citrus, herbs, spices, and other teas.

## *Citrus*

We saw earlier one of the common additions you can make to bring a little citrus into your tea. Lemon is an excellent example of citrus you can add to your tea blend. While you can get a similar effect by adding lemon juice to your steeped cup, adding lemon before it has been brewed means you don't have to add it later, and for many, that means you just add water, and the tea is done! Blending citrus into your tea can add a pleasant zest to your cup, or it can mix with some of the more subtle flavors and enhance them.

An interesting effect of adding lemon to your tea is that the brew will be lighter in color due to a chemical reaction between the acid in the lemon and the tea itself.

**Tip #46: Add citrus to an herbal tea for extra vitamin C and help with congestion or a sore throat. The flavor will also be pleasant, and if you are having trouble tasting anything, many citrus fruits have a strong flavor that can come through.**

**Tip #47: Add citrus to a black tea for a subtle zingy background flavor. Many black teas have deep, intense flavors, and a little dash of something completely different, like citrus, can accentuate those flavors.**

Some common citrus ingredients are listed below

- Lemon peel
- Orange peel
- Grapefruit peel
- Dried pineapple (though not technically citrus, the flavor profile is similar)
- Kumquat peel

## _Herbs_

Herbal teas are their own thing, but using herbs to make your own blend can give you completely different flavors than the herbal teas themselves. Lavender is a common flavor enhancer for tea blends, and it's also a deceptively strong flavor itself.

**Tip #48: Herbs may have mellow flavors, but they can also quickly dominate a brew. Licorice is a great example of the strength of herbal flavors. Licorice root is common enough in teas, and just a little can lend a powerful flavor, but the right amount can add a wholesome warmth to your tea, and it's good for you!**

When you begin making herbal blends think both about the flavor you're looking for and the effect you want. Many herbs have health benefits, and some can change the texture tea leaves behind, so choose accordingly. Adding herbs may also change how your tea reacts to the flavors you add after it has been brewed. Mint tea, in particular, can quickly grow syrupy with added sugar, but adding mint to a chocolate tea can give you a cup that tastes exactly like a certain seasonally available mint chocolate cookie.

**Tip #49: Add ginger to your tea for a savory, spicy undertone. Dried ginger can be found in most grocery stores, and it's good for your digestion.**

**Tip #50: If you want to make a blend but only have tea bags, you still can! Measure out the flavors you would blend with your tea, and either put them in their own little baggie or mix them in a large container you can quickly fill an infuser from.**

Some common herbal ingredients are listed below

- Lavender
- Ginger
- Licorice root
- Mint
- Rosemary

## *Spices*

Your spice rack is your friend when you're making your own tea blends, particularly if you have a few tasty ingredients. Spices live an interesting double life because some work only in blends, some work only if you add them once the tea has brewed, others can do both, and many of them shouldn't come within 30 yards of your teacup.

**Tip #51: When making a blend, creativity is great, but don't get carried away. Some flavors that are delicious in food do not mix well with most teas. Smoked paprika, for example, will likely not pair with many teas.**

When you pick the spices you want to add to your tea, an interesting thing you have to consider is how they will remain with your tea. If you're packaging your own tea bags, this is less of a problem because they can contain fine powders. However, if you're using an infuser, most powdered spices will not stay in place in a large package of tea, so you'll be left with almost none of the spice you picked out. To that end, look for whole spices rather than powdered form. Cinnamon sticks rather than ground cinnamon. Whole dried herbs instead of their ground counterparts, seeds instead of crushed flavor shrapnel.

**Tip #52: Research fun herbs and flavor combinations to use because some may surprise you. Catnip is actually a common ingredient in tea, and it can be great as a supplement to an already-sleepy tea.**

Some common spices you can add to your blend are listed below

- Cardamom
- Cloves
- Nutmeg
- Vanilla bean
- Cinnamon

## *Other Teas*

This one is cheating a little bit, but there's nothing wrong with skipping the long search for ingredients and just combining a few of your favorite teas. One of my favorite summer teas is just a combination of hibiscus rose tea with a, particularly sour orange tea, chilled and served with a lemon wedge.

**Tip #53: Tea jail does not exist. You can make the tea you want; however you want.**

There are a few things you can do to make a blend of multiple teas. If your teas come in sachets, you can just tear them open and mix them before putting them in an infuser or into two new sachets. Be careful to keep the portions consistent because it's easy to accidentally create an overpoweringly strong cup from a few strong teas.

If your teas are loose-leaf, then there's no problem. Combine them and put them in an infuser like you would any other tea.

**Tip #54: Keep ratios in mind when you make a blend of multiple teas. If one tea is particularly strong or has a flavor you enjoy, you may want more or less of it in the mix. If both teas are strong, then aim to keep them equal. A precise scale can be your friend while you do this.**

If the teas you want to blend are bagged, there are a few more things you can do. The first option is the easiest: heat a larger container and brew them both simultaneously. Keep track of separate brewing times if you do this, and then pour yourself a cup when they're done. Alternatively, you can open and mix the bags before carefully repacking them into your own teabags. If you do this, make sure the bag is adequately sealed to keep your blend fresh

**Tip #55: If you have to open a tea bag, do it over a plate or a large paper towel. The tea powder is fine and will get lost, and some tea stains when it gets wet.**

Below are some complementary blends of two types of tea

- Earl Grey and Jasmine
- Masala Chai and Chocolate
- Chamomile and Catnip
- Macha and Lavender

# *Chapter Review*

- Tea is not static. You can blend and mix your tea with all kinds of different flavors to form something new and unique to your preferences
- Though there are as many types of tea blends as there are flavors to blend them with, we can categorize some of the most common tea blends under citrus, herbs, spices, and other teas
- Citrus often uses parts of citrus fruits
- Herbs use full, dried herbs
- Spices use large pieces of unground spices

Other teas can be blended by taking directly from the bag, sachet, or loose-leaf mixture and simply mixing them at a ratio you find appealing.

# Chapter 6: A Brief Look At Tea Etiquette

## *Cultural Heathen*

The first time I made tea as an adult, it was in the small hours of the night, and I did it while sitting at a desk I found on a street corner. There was not a saucer in sight. I often stirred my tea with the back of a pen and just kind of hoped it wouldn't leak ink into my delightful little blue cup. When I finally learned about scones, I immediately tried dipping one into my tea.

When I was taught at the university, I used to bring tea and cookies on the last day of class. I would bring my kettle, enough tea for everyone to have 2 or 3 cups, and more cookies than anyone could consider reasonable. My students also brought treats and snacks, and we made a little party of it.

However, in all that mirth and joy was a sour blight, or so I was told. My students weren't exactly posh. I taught in Arizona, not exactly the high seat of sophistication in the world. However, I could usually get the better part of a room to recoil because I dared to dip a cookie into my tea. The humanity! Clearly, this was the untoward action of a woman mad with power, emblematic of a rotten soul, likely corrupt since the first day of class.

The first time I did it, the recoil I heard from my students was enough to make me want to do it even more. I started making a point of dipping a single cookie in my tea at the end of every semester to see if I could get the same reaction. And because it was delicious. Invariably, I would get the same response every semester. A single dip, a gasp, an exclamation of contempt. A student might point a finger, proclaiming that I "am a wicked old dragon, rotten to the core, deserve to be removed from my position and thrown into a landfill with the other refuse." I'm paraphrasing, but that was the general idea.

People drink tea worldwide, and they drink it for different reasons and with varying weights. Some people drink it for utility and enjoyment; that's me. Others do it as a cultural or religious ceremony. Others do it because it's just part of life, like dinner or nap times. Many do it for a combination of the reasons above or for ones outside those boundaries. In short, tea is a loaded beverage. People have expectations and investments in it, and I tend to have absolutely none of those.

My students, it seemed, lived in a mixture of cultural and physical revulsion at my heathenism. Some of them didn't like my dipping because it just wasn't done, and others thought it just looked kind of yucky.

Though they aren't as overt, Americans have ceremony and convention for their tea, even more so for coffee, but they're so ingrained into practice that they don't seem like ceremony and instead just seem like the right way to do things. Other countries and cultures are much more overt about their tea. This chapter will take a superficial look at some of the tea etiquette of different cultures, with the consistent acknowledgment that the rites and ceremonies described are essential aspects of cultures I am not part of, but that doesn't make them any less valuable. It is important to point out that I couldn't hope to talk about the tea rituals of every country or people who love tea. So this chapter will simply touch on a few interesting tidbits from around the world with the acknowledgment that this is just the top of the teabag, rather than a deep-diving exploration.

It's also essential to point out the difference between etiquette and common practice.

**Etiquette**: What's considered proper or polite; adheres to tradition and ceremony.

**Practice**: What people tend actually to do

Tea etiquette does not extend to every home and every tea drinker. If every person followed every etiquette rule for each cup of tea, it would take considerably longer to drink it, and nobody would get anything else done. With that in mind...


## *United States Tea and Coffee Etiquette*

I was initially tempted to call this section "American" Tea and Coffee Etiquette, but I realized that would be too vague and a misnomer. The United States as a nation is built on Native American land, so any section named American Tea Etiquette would have to account for the diverse ceremonies and rites unique to each Native American tribe.

That being said, the US itself has its own unspoken social rules for coffee, and those rules also extend to tea. Like many things in the US, the social rules are unstated, and the enforcement of those rules is not stringent. If you break a rule, it won't be overtly acknowledged as a broken rule, but what you're doing may be called odd, and you may get some sidelong glances. For example, we can return to my cookie dipped in my tea. I wasn't called improper, just odd and unsavory. If you live in the United States and want evidence that etiquette around hot drinks is alive and well in the US, order a coffee and ask for a dash of cayenne on the top or sit at a table and enjoy a mate, which is generally served in a metal-lined gourd. Nobody will walk up and say, "you're going to drink jail," but someone may remark that what you're doing is very out of the ordinary.

A cursory glance at the etiquette

- Flavor black tea with some manner of cream (or dairy substitute), sugar (or substitute), or lemon juice
- Tea is served plain unless otherwise specified so the drinker can flavor it themselves
- Do not loudly slurp your tea
- Iced drinks are served with a straw

**Tip #56: If you are drinking your tea in a cafe, particularly a crowded one, you should leave as soon as you are finished and have paid your bill. The expectation is that you are done with**

your table once you have completed your order. If you intend to be there longer, order another drink.

## *British Afternoon Tea*

Afternoon tea is a light meal served with tea. It is common to eat small sandwiches and pastries, generally taken between 3 and 5 PM. Afternoon tea started in the mid 19th century by the Duchess of Bedford, who wanted a light meal a few hours before dinner. As with anything associated with royalty, it quickly developed firm rules that were just as quickly ignored by most of the populace. However, the etiquette lives on for more formal afternoon teas.

A cursory glance at the etiquette

- Add milk only once the tea has finished brewing
- Hold your teacup by the handle with the thumb and forefingers
- Stir gently and place the spoon on your saucer once you are done with it
- Do not sip from the spoon like you would a soup
- Do not dunk your biscuits into your tea

**Tip #57: There is a myth that it is proper to hold your pinkie finger out like a tiny biological antenna while drinking your afternoon tea. That is untrue and is something of a faux pas to perpetuate. However, teacup**

**handles are small, and you likely won't have room for your pinkie finger anyway, so just let it rest without pointing it willy nilly.**

Again, if you walk into most British homes during afternoon tea, you won't likely see each of these rules being followed, far from it, but etiquette lives separately from daily practice. So don't worry if you simply cannot battle the urge to dunk your biscuit into your tea. You more than likely won't be alone.

## *Chinese Tea*

The Gong Fu style of brewing tea comes from China, and with it also comes a standard set of steps to evoke the best possible taste from tea. China has a massive tea culture, and the Chinese tea ceremony is even a part of traditional Chinese weddings. We are not looking at the traditional Chinese tea ceremony. We are instead discussing Gong Fu brewing because this text is about making the best cup of tea, not making the best marriage, and there is etiquette to the steps of Gong Fu brewing, just as there is etiquette in every step of the Chinese tea ceremony.

Here is a cursory glance at the etiquette

- First, warm your teapot, which should be small. Warm it with boiling water, then discard the water to make room for tea.
- Fill the pot with tea leaves and rinse them with boiling water.
- Brew your tea by pouring water into the pot.

- Pour the tea into a pitcher so the flavors can mingle, then pour from the pitcher into small teacups.
- Repeat the process by adding more hot water to the pot as needed until your leaves are spent.

**Tip #58: Many tea leaves are strong enough for multiple steepings like those typically used in Gong Fu brewing. Try re-steeping your loose leaf tea once or twice. You may be surprised by how strong the second brewing will still be.**

## *Chapter Review*

- For many people, tea is part of their cultural and spiritual lives.
- For others, tea is just a beloved drink
- And for many people, both are true.
- Tea is enjoyed around the world, and with that comes many different formal rules for drinking it, but those rules are also often readily disregarded in favor of casual enjoyment.

# Chapter 7: Common Misconceptions

## *Every Mistake I've Ever Made*

As we discussed in Chapter 6, many of the rules and practices surrounding tea go unspoken. That means many people are not initiated into the best practices for brewing tea and are left to discover it on their own. That's what I had to do. It means two things: 1) There is an underlying assumption that everyone can learn to make tea, and 2) many people make terrible tea.

When I first started drinking tea, I often wondered why some cups turned out so bitter while others barely had any flavor at all. I'd go through the motions making a cup of tea, heating the water, steeping a bag, then I'd go back to work. It took me a few months to realize the bitterness of my tea directly corresponded with how long I was taking between breaks. It took longer still for me to understand; all I had to do was take the teabag out of the cup once it had brewed for a set amount of time. Every time I see a student with a travel mug and a dangling tea label, I shudder for the bitter mess they must be carrying, but maybe they like it. Or perhaps they added enough sweetener and cream that the type of tea within is insignificant.

One of the most consistent missteps I made that I've seen repeated by others has to do with sweetener. I don't have the biggest sweet tooth, but on occasion, I like to have a nice sweet tea as a celebration for finishing a big project. When I used to make myself a sweeter tea, I noticed that the texture would slightly change as I made it. I'd have my cup, nice and steamy, and my little spoon and a jar of sugar. I'd pour a little sugar, stir it, taste it, and pour a little more. The sweeter I wanted my tea, the more I'd have to reconcile that something about the texture would just be off.

One of the easiest liquid sweeteners you can make is simple syrup. All you have to do is add sugar to water, dissolve it, and let it simmer. Simple syrup is, as the name denotes, a syrup, and it's very easy to make, including by accident. While sweetening your tea, keep an eye on how much sweetener you're adding and how hot your tea is. If you like your tea nearly boiling like me, then you may accidentally be making tea-flavored simple syrup, which is delicious but isn't the most nutritious use of your time. If you want to avoid this fate, either make and sweeten a larger batch or just let your tea cool below boiling before adding sweetener. Some teas will still get thicker, but you won't stray as quickly into syrup territory.

For as many types of tea and methods of brewing it, there are an equal or greater number of ways you can end up drinking a bitter mistake. Some tea misconceptions are minor things that you'd barely notice unless you had been making and drinking tea for a long time. Other errors are likely the reason some people claim they hate all kinds of tea.

Every mistake outlined within this chapter is something I have done, often multiple times, and in some cases, while making a cup for other people--the worst cases. It's worth noting that tea etiquette is wildly specific, varies from culture to culture, is extremely important to some people, and will not be even remotely touched upon in this chapter. Ceremonies relating to tea are their own organism with rules passed down in some cases for thousands of years, and it's also just not something I've encountered while making tea from the kettle in the bottom drawer of my desk.

## *Errors Before Brewing*

The process leading up to brewing your tea is as essential as any other stage. Picking the proper tea for your needs and making sure you have the correct apparatus are crucial. There is also ample room for things to go wrong here.

To prevent most errors that occur before brewing, be mindful of your decisions and the tea you select. If your tea comes from a box, read the box. You'll find essential directions there, including brewing times, temperatures, and sometimes even optimal water content. If you're making tea yourself, then you're old enough to read the box the tea is coming from, so these kinds of mistakes are quite avoidable. Generally, if you're thinking about every decision you make when you're leading up to making your tea, things should go well. Most of the mistakes I have made were due to thoughtlessness and sleep deprivation. One does not try to steep a packet of sugar when they are of sound mind.

Tea is a little different than coffee and other beverages in that you can be very involved in the brewing process, or you can be mostly hands-off. If you think you aren't in a mindset to pay attention, then just throw a bag into some hot water and count down the clock. If you're too tired to focus, then that wouldn't be the best time to start measuring out some loose leaf tea.

**Tip #59: Do not rely on herbal teas for a boost of caffeine because they have none. Chamomile, the quintessential sleepy tea, is an herbal tea, and most other herbal teas have similar somniferous influence, or at best, they just won't wake you up.**

**Tip #60: Combining teas, whether by steeping two bags or mixing different loose-leaf blends, can result in some delicious and energizing brews. Or you will find that your two favorite teas combined are overpowering and overly pungent. Combining two black teas may result in a stronger, richer mixture, but it can also give you a muddled caffeinated experience with no gain in flavor.**

**Tip #61: If you're going to combine tea bags, use a bigger container to brew them in. Teabags are generally filled to a level that would infuse a full cup of water. Adding two tea bags to one cup will, sensibly, make an overpowering cup of tea.**

# *Brewing Errors*

Brewing your tea is the time when something is most likely to go awry. With so much to consider, from temperature to brewing time, it's easy to miss something and end up with a subpar cup. Mistakes I made were generally due to never supposing that different teas brew in different ways. It led me to steep a strong jasmine tea for as long as I might an herbal brew. What that gave me was an agonizingly bitter drink that tasted vaguely of jasmine.

**Tip #62: Do not squeeze the last drops of flavor out of the bag when you are done steeping. While it looks like you are wringing delicious morsels of flavor from your expended tea bag, what you're really doing is depositing a healthy dusting of dregs at the bottom of your cup. If you find your white cups are tinted brown after your morning mug of earl grey, that is more than likely why. The dregs can also stain clothes, furniture, and even your teeth, so stay away.**

**Tip #63: Do not dunk your teabag. While brewing a bag of tea, the label may seem like a tantalizing toy to dip and immerse your bag and get every drop of flavor out quicker, but it doesn't actually do anything other than creating a spill risk. If you need to pass the time while you brew your tea, find something unrelated to your cup to occupy yourself because dunking your bag doesn't help the flavor and has been the reason for many spilled cups.**

Tip #64: Leaving your tea to steep too long. Obey the directions on the box or do your research before brewing. Leaving your tea to steep for too long will ruin the flavor. Though the aesthetic of the tea label hanging gently from the rim of your mug is pleasant, for frequent tea drinkers, it's more of an announcement that you aren't enjoying your cup as much as you could be.

Tip #65: Most teas should be brewed once the water has stopped boiling. There are some exceptions, but most teas should begin steeping once your water has stilled and reached a level temperature. Brewing your tea in actively boiling water can burn it and sour the delicate flavors, and some tea bags are flimsy themselves and can come open with too much jostling.

Tip #66: Heating your water with the tea already in it. As a rule, unless otherwise specified, only add your tea once the water has reached the necessary temperature. Throwing some tea into cold water and then bringing it to a boil will result in over steeping, burned tea, and often a torn bag.

Tip #67: Add flavor enhancers after the brew is finished. If you add honey or cream while the tea is steeping or while the water is boiling, the tea will not infuse the water the same as if it were clean. Give your tea fewer obstacles to work around.

**Tip #68: Reuse (some of) your teabags. Many teas are strong enough to be steeped multiple times. Experiment with your favorites to see if the flavor still meets your expectations after a re-steeping. If it does, you've doubled or tripled how many cups of tea you can have!**

## *Drinking Errors*

Drinking tea is a pretty self-explanatory process. If you're at the point in life where you can read a book, you're likely more than a little experienced with consuming liquids. By the time I was making my own tea, I would have even considered myself an expert on beverage consumption. That being said, expertise in consuming liquids isn't the only prerequisite for drinking good tea. There are some misconceptions people commonly have that are adjacent to the literal drinking of tea.

**Tip #69: Avoid drinking your tea while it is brewing. The water will be hot, and the tea will be weak, and nothing overall is gained from drinking your tea before it is ready.**

**Tip #70: Avoid saturating your tea with milk or cream. Some teas, like masala chai, do well with more milk. Others cannot fully steep if the water is too clogged with milk, or worse, they can steep all you want, but you'll still only taste what you added.**

**Tip #71: Too much sugar can make your tea syrupy. Simple syrup is a combination of 1 part water with 1 part sugar. Dissolve the sugar in hot water, let cool, and you have a thick sweet, simple syrup. Tea is hot water that often cools, and if you add too much sugar, you're going to get a lot closer to drinking simple syrup than you want to.**

## *A Note on Tea Misconceptions*

If you enjoy the tea you brew, then continue enjoying it the way you always have. I regularly still make a mistake while brewing my favorite tea, earl grey, but that mistake has become a deliberate part of my tea. Black teas brew hot, and I tend to brew mine significantly hotter and drink them while they're borderline steam. I like my black tea at a temperature that can make my glasses fog from a good 6 inches away.

The lessons included in this chapter are common technical missteps, but if you enjoy the tea you make, even if you make it different from the standard, continue making it how you like. Starbucks features the sweetest, most milky masala chai I've ever encountered, but millions of people enjoy it every day. That pleasure is not wrong, even if the flavor of the tea comes through the layers of milk and cream more subtly than many prefer.

If it brings you endless satisfaction to still squeeze the dregs from your tea bag, then continue to do so while also possibly investing in some high-strength dish cleaner and toothpaste. In a similar vein, if you enjoy having hot tea and iced tea happen in the same cup over a few hours, then what is a mistake for some is a bonus for you. Enjoy it.

## *Chapter Review*

- A drink as widely consumed as tea is bound to come with a few common misconceptions.
- Many of the misconceptions surrounding tea occur before making it, during the actual brewing process, and while drinking it.
- However, if the way you enjoy your tea falls under one of the misconceptions described in this chapter, that doesn't mean you're making your tea wrong or need to change it. It just means you have a style.

# Chapter 8: Using What You Know

## *How Will You Make Your Tea?*

If every cup of tea I make goes through every possible step I could take to make tea; I wouldn't have time to drink it. I wouldn't have time to do anything. My cats would miss me, and I'd be evicted from my home because all I would have time to do is make tea. There would be times that, by the time I finished brewing and drinking one cup, I'd need to start the next one. The brewing cycle and drinking and brewing and drinking would be functionally endless because of how much tea I drink and how many ways there are to spend a good long time making the stuff.

When I make tea, I tend to make it in one of three ways. These three types of tea making capture a few of the different methods discussed in earlier chapters, and some of them rely on the exact techniques I have openly said to avoid. Tea is a drink of nuance, and in that nuance, there is even room for total, flagrant hypocrisy.

The three ways I make tea correspond to how much effort or time I'm willing to put into the whole process. It tends to depend on how busy I am, how long of a tea break I'm ready to take, or just how willing I am to dedicate myself to making a beverage I'm going to finish within a few minutes anyway. In short, my tea-making generally corresponds to how lazy or productive I'm feeling.

## *Highest Effort*

At my most productive, most industrious, and tea-enthusiastic, I go through every available step. It is when I'm making tea for the joy of making tea. It can be such a relaxing, comforting process. The smell of the herbs and oils, the texture of the cup and honey, the sound of rustling loose leaf tea as I fill an infuser or pack a teabag. I don't make tea cocktails because making tea is already intoxicating enough.

I don't often make tea like this on workdays, and if I do, it takes up my entire break. The time spent heating the water perfectly, making my own blend, or measuring out a pre-made mix is precise work, especially if you do it by sight and without a scale. You are never obligated to make tea in any way that doesn't suit your desire, but I would recommend taking the time to work through every single possible step just once to see how much joy you can derive from it. There is something profoundly meditative about making tea-the smells, the connection with billions of people who have loved the drink just the same, the knowledge that you'll have created something beautiful at the end. It's a wonderful feeling.

It also takes forever. Really. I've spent a full hour making one batch of tea because I wanted to be absolutely precise with the blend I was making. I ended up even taking the time to crush some herbs in a mortar and pestle to sprinkle into the cup, and that decadence is an investment in time you should not expect of yourself for every cup or every day.

## *Medium Effort*

When I want tea, I know I'm going to enjoy it but don't want to invest a huge amount of time into making it; this is the brewing process I use. It is the middle ground between maximum and minimum effort, and I find it most frequently fits with how much I want tea and how much I want to get back to whatever I was doing—probably petting a cat. It's usually petting a cat that I'm returning to.

My medium effort brewing method is simple but still brings out good flavors from my tea. It is the method focused most on the result, not the process, whereas the highest effort method was focused on enjoying the process and getting a payoff in the form of a beautiful product.

When I want to put a little effort into my tea, I generally use pre-mixed tea. Whether that's coming from bags I've bought or filled when I was feeling more industrious doesn't matter. The point is that I don't go to extra effort to prepare what is going into the cup or pot. Loose-leaf doesn't really factor into this type of brewing unless it's a blend I've used a lot and can scoop quickly. Jasmine pearl is an excellent example of a loose leaf that fits in this category. The wonderful thing about Jasmine pearl is that the tea is already condensed into these lovely little spheres, so they're really easy to measure. I know that I enjoy a cup of tea if it has been brewed for 2.5 minutes and contains anywhere from 6-8 pearls. That's a quick measurement. I would not do the same for a loose leaf tea I'm less familiar with. Sorry, Oolong, you're all too different, so I'm saving you for when I'm feeling more energetic.

To heat water for this kind of brewing, I use whatever electric kettle is around. If it doesn't have precise temperature control, that's fine. I just estimate by letting the water cool a bit after the kettle has gone off naturally. Teas do have specific temperatures they brew best at, but as long as you aren't burning your tea, you'll still usually get something serviceable in your cup even if your temperature is off.

## *Minimum Effort*

Tea can be a journey. It can be an adventure through steps and avenues of flavor and fragrances that make the process worth the work before you ever reach the end. Tea can be a journey. It can also be a destination because sometimes you just really want something hot to drink because you've been awake for far too long and working harder than you think a person ought ever to need to work, and something caffeinated would just really hit the spot.

Sometimes we make tea for the function it provides. The utili-tea, if you will. Many teas are caffeinated, and many more can be mixed well with other energizing beverages. In college, one of my favorite drinks was a chai latte with a shot of espresso. As the years wore on, I'd add more espresso, but it would still be tea, just tea that exists entirely to serve a purpose. The drink was so bitter that it would be undrinkable to all but the truly desperate.

When I'm making tea entirely for the result and not the process, I tend to break virtually every one of the rules outlined in the previous chapters. I use whatever heat source is available. Microwave? Fine, it'll do. Campfire? Great, my kettle might be black now, but at least the water is hot. The only source of heat I've got is an oven? Ok, sure, I guess my kettle is technically metal and can last in there without warping.

I use whatever is present to get the water to the point that it is hot enough for the flavors in the tea to diffuse into the water. At this point, exact temperatures are so distant from my mind that it would feel silly if someone asked if my cup was at the proper 180 degrees F.

It is also the time where I start adding flavors recklessly. Like a child with a t-shirt cannon, I blast flavors into my tea wildly, barely considering anything but making a drink that is palatable and gets the job done. It is how I discovered both that I absolutely detest soy milk and that the flavor of soy milk can be covered if you dump a packet of hot chocolate into your Earl Grey.

You might find yourself making tea like this. You might even do it often. That's fine if you do, so long as you enjoy it or it does what you need it to. As important as tea is to the world, it's a drink. It doesn't care if you can't taste every floral note in the herbal medley dancing within your sachet.

I outline these tea brewing methods not to say any is better than the other, but to pay special attention to the different purposes, we can have when making tea. This chapter will put in order all the steps that have been broken down and discussed in the rest of this book. We will outline every possible action you can take to make a maximum effort cup, but we will do that with the necessary caveat that this isn't the only proper way to make tea, just one way to do it among many.

## Making The Maximum Effort

There is a certain mindset that lends itself perfectly to putting every effort into making the perfect cup of tea. It's when you want something beautiful, but you also want to go through the process of making it. It's like when you don't just want to see a pretty painting; you want to make it too. You don't just want to eat; you want to cook. You want to write as much as you want to have written.

When you don't just want to drink a beautiful cup of tea, you want to make it too; that's when it's time to put the maximum effort in. That's when you bust out the measuring spoons, the good infusers that aren't stained with a patina of a million other brews. When you finally crack open that jar of honey you bought at the farmers market because it looked pretty and didn't have a price tag. The one with a bit of actual honeycomb inside it. It is the moment you finally use the honey that you had to budget after buying.

The previous chapters have been an exercise in the theoretical. Seven chapters of "if" and "then." The remainder of this chapter will put into practice that theoretical knowledge by working through the entire process of making the ideal cup of tea, with the essential caveat that "ideal" is both subjective to the individual and to the tea that being made.

Because it's my favorite, we'll be looking at how to make the "perfect" cup of Earl Grey tea from leaf selection down to which cream we could add. While this process won't produce the perfect cup for every person, the framework stands. The content of each step may differ, but the actions themselves will more than likely stay the same. You might not add almond milk to a chamomile tea, but it's a good idea to take a step to consider what flavors you could add to enhance your brew.

Let's begin.


## *Step 1: Selecting Your Leaf*

If I want a good Earl Grey, I generally don't even entertain the idea of bags or sachets. The reason is that Earl Grey is flavored from dried bergamot oranges and through an infusion of the oil from a bergamot peel. That means the flavors, while strong, are a bit delicate.

Bagged tea, as we discussed, is often ground to a powder. Picture a beautiful oil painting-a resplendent work of artistry. Now grind it into a powder. Technically, the paint is still there, but it's not where it should be. When tea is ground, the flavors can't cling as well to the leaves because the leaves don't exist anymore.

So, if I'm looking for a good Earl Grey, I generally go for loose leaf. It leaves more room for customization later, lets you see and smell what exactly you're getting without worrying about any of it shooting up your nose, and it's easier to change how strong of a brew you'll get. I like a strong tea.

I generally shop local for my loose leaf tea, and that's what I'd recommend if it's possible. Find a tea shop near you, if there is one, and buy the leaves they recommend. The reason for this is that you then know exactly where your tea is coming from, you know it hasn't been in a warehouse for six years gathering dust, and you support a local business.

If you can't find a local tea shop and your only recourse is to order online, then there are two brands I'd recommend specifically for Earl Grey. Windsor Castle and Harney & Sons are both pretty good quality tea, with my preference being toward Windsor. Both are loose leaf teas, and with Windsor, you can easily see the difference between the tea leaves and the citrus peel, and that's just a lovely thing to know. A benefit of Harney & Sons is that their tea comes in a cute tin you can reuse. I still use one to store other teas in.

In summary, buy a good loose leaf tea where you can see the difference between leaves and peel, and shop local if you can.

## *Step 2: Making a Blend*

I love plain Earl Grey. The flavors are brash and delicious, and it always just feels like the quintessential tea to me. But I also love how many flavors can complement this incredible tea, and we're talking about making the absolute best cup, not a good cup.

Step 2 is to make a blend, and that can mostly only be done with a loose leaf tea. With our Earl Grey, there are a few common blending ingredients that work well. The first is lavender. When I make a blend of Earl Grey, I usually add a little lavender because it adds such a clear floral note, a vibrant purple flower peeking up from a loamy forest floor.

I would also recommend vanilla, with the necessary disclaimer that vanilla is a strong flavor. It only takes two vanilla beans to make half a gallon of ice cream, and your single pot of tea isn't going to take nearly as much flavoring. If you use vanilla, do it sparingly because even a tiny bit more than you need will give you Earl Grey-flavored vanilla water.

In a teaspoon of loose leaf Earl Grey, I typically only add three lavender flowers because I like the flavor to be subtle. If I'm adding vanilla, I will usually chop a tiny piece of the vanilla pod and distribute it among a tablespoon of tea. Vanilla is strong, and if you look at the reviews for almost any Earl Grey vanilla tea, you'll find a horde of people saying the flavor was overpowering.

The real key to making a blend is experimenting. You're going to make a lot of teas you don't like. That's part of the fun. If you're enjoying the process of making the tea, an unsatisfactory result doesn't sour the process. It just means you get to do it again.

## *Step 3: Gathering Appropriate Apparatus*

If you're going through all this trouble to make the best tea you can, you probably don't want just one cup. When I'm going through the effort of making my own blend, I'll usually make myself a large pot of tea, and that's what I'd recommend doing. If you don't have a teapot, find one. They're everywhere. You can't stumble through Walmart without seeing a few. If you've been within a thousand feet of a thrift store, then you've been in close proximity to a throng of delightful and unique teapots. If you find one, you love that has a tiny chip, all the better because your pot has personali-tea.

But you won't just need a teapot. If you're really getting into making your tea, you're going to need:

- An electric kettle
- An infuser
- A decanter for honey or other additives

84

- A spoon
- A cup
- A cute little saucer for your cup
- And the teapot, which we've discussed

**Your kettle** should have temperature customization. Most good ones do, and that's essential if you want to get the most flavor out of your tea without scalding it. I would recommend metal or opaque glass kettles for two reasons. They're going to resist warping much better than their plastic counterparts. And if you can't see inside them, you won't have to confront just how quickly the calcium from your water builds up in there. Within a few months of use, my first kettle had a sheet of white rock covering the heating surface, and that's just more than you want to contend with when you're trying to make something delicious.

**Your infuser** should fit the tea you're brewing. Literally, your tea needs to fit in there. That means it should be able to close without any tea getting caught in the hinges. You also want to look for one with small enough holes that the tea can't get out but big enough that the water can get in. If the head of a thumbtack fits in the hole, you'll likely be good. If the entire tack can go through, consider finding one a little finer.

**Your decanter** should be designed for whatever it's decanting. If you're going to be using honey for your tea, look for a special container for your honey. You'll want one that doesn't have a twisting lid, or if it does, the cover is far away from where the honey is. The reason for that is because honey gets everywhere. Just ask bees. The stuff is all over their homes. Honey or any sweet, sugar-based liquid can get into cracks, lids, and any other tiny space. There, it'll dry, but it will leave a deposit. For honey, that slowly builds up until you have a lid you basically need a bodybuilder to remove. For other sweet liquids, you're going to struggle until you shatter the buildup of sugar crystals.

**Your spoon** should be small, relatively narrow, and with a long handle. It's strange to consider spoon design, but we're putting every effort into this, and spoon design can change things a little bit. A spoon with a long handle will dip into any cup without getting your filthy, filthy hands into the precious, delicate brew. It means you can stir honey or sugar easily. The ladle of the spoon should be relatively narrow because if it's too wide, it'll just scoop up whatever you've got in the bottom rather than getting it to move and dissolve. A bonus of having a nice little spoon is that you can clink it against your teacup if you need to get someone's attention in the most forceful yet polite way possible. Nobody can ignore a dedicated spoon tapper.

**Your cup** should be shallow enough that it can only hold a little tea that you will finish before it grows cold. Or, if you want a deep cup, it should be heat resistant to keep relatively steady the temperature of your tea. The cup is arguably one of the most critical pieces of equipment when it comes to tea because it's really hard to drink straight from the pot. I prefer a deep cup because I drink a lot of tea, and I always find that if I use a small one, it is inevitable that my cup runneth over. Beyond depth, find a cup with either a good handle or one that has a perfectly shaped saucer to keep it steady. Tea, generally, is hot, and you don't want to burn your hands.

**Your saucer** should be perfectly shaped to the bottom of your cup. If you need a saucer, then you need a good one. Using a saucer that doesn't fit your cup is just going to make the whole thing slide and slosh around, and it'll be worse than if you'd set the cup on your head. A perfectly sized saucer will hug the base of your cup and make it much easier to balance. Then, you can lift that closer to your face so your hot cup will have less distance to travel. Think of the saucer as a ship, a vessel that shall transport the precious cargo of your tea wherever you need it. The ship must be able to hold the load, or everything will sink. You don't see anybody stuffing an entire museum onto a rowboat. Your saucer should be able to fly easily toward you, holding tight the cup, its cargo.

**Your teapot** should be short and stout, tall and thin, angular and confusing. There are a million styles of teapots, and you should select one that does two jobs flawlessly because it only really has two jobs. It should be made of something relatively heat resistant. Your pot needs to keep your tea safe through travels between tables and chairs, counters, and couches. Ceramic, clay, and cast iron are good materials to look for. The second job of any teapot is to look good. You're building an atmosphere, so find the pot that fits you just as well as it does the tea.

## *Step 4: Steeping*

You have your apparatus set up. The water is hot. For a black tea like Earl Grey, that means it's around 200 degrees F. The next step is the most obvious one. Take your filled infuser and submerge it in hot water. If the water was recently boiling, take a tiny step back when you put your tea in because the water can surge back up, and getting burned is a great way to ruin a peaceful evening making tea.

Leave your tea submerged in the water for the appropriate time. It varies depending on the tea. For Earl Grey, you'll need to leave the tea in the water for three to five minutes, depending on how strong you like your tea. The water should quickly develop a deep brown color. Resist the temptation to stir, dip, or press your tea. Some infusers have mechanisms that will wring the last bits of moisture out of the leaves, and you're going to want to avoid those like they're your least favorite coworker at a company picnic. What you get by pressing your tea is a big burst of dregs and tannins. Both can stain your cup, clothes, and teeth, and both are also quite bitter.

Don't touch the infuser until the brewing time is up. Once it has passed, gently lift the infuser out of the cup. Be gentle because you don't want to shake any leaves into the water that may now be flexible enough to slip through even small gaps in your infuser. Also, the water is still hot, and teacups are a no-splash zone.

## *Step 5: Enhancing the Flavor*

Once you've steeped your tea, it's technically done, but we aren't stopping at technically. If we ended things at the technicality line, technically, you could chew on a tea bag and drink hot water and call the results tea.

I like to add cream and sweetener to my Earl Grey, and the ratios are entirely subjective, so this is another part of the process that takes trial and error. Delicious trial and error. If you're adding a sweetener like honey, sugar, Splenda, anything like that, then it is often a good idea to add that first. There are cultural and social rules in many places that dictate the order you should go in, but if you're strictly going for flavor, it makes sense to put the things that dissolve better in hot liquid first while the drink is hot. Most creams and liquid flavors are cold, and if you like a lot of them, sugar and honey will just rest at the bottom of your cup, so add the sweets first. Stir them with your perfectly long and narrow spoon until they've dissolved. If you're doing honey, then you should be able to feel the bottom of the cup with your spoon to know if all the honey is gone. If you're using sugar, the same thing, but give the cup a second to rest once you finish stirring and check again. Sugar is tiny, tasty, and gets swept up in the vigor of your spooning, so give it a second to settle. Check it. If there's nothing grainy at the bottom, then you're good.

For your creams, add them sparingly and by the cup unless you're confident in your measurements. Better to try again with a single cup than a full pot. I like almond milk in my Earl Grey, so I generally add about a tablespoon of that to a 12 oz cup of tea. Stir. Pay attention to the color. Color is one of the easiest ways to consistently know if you've added too much or too little cream. Again, it's subjective, so pay attention if you like a sawdust tan or a creamy beige.

# Step 6: Drink it

This step doesn't require much explanation. If you know how to make tea, you should know how to drink a liquid. Do pay attention to the heat of your brew, though. Often your cup may seem cool, but the tea inside is still scalding.

**Tip #72: Drink your tea when it is ready. Take a moment to enjoy the tea you've made when it's ready to be appreciated because there is no better time for tea.**

Beyond that, just enjoy your tea. The end of the brewing process may seem anticlimactic after all that buildup, but the point wasn't to make something better than the steps that created it. We go to so much effort to make tea when we want to enjoy the work and the tea. The drink you make should be good. It's tea, and you've done so much to make it your own, so it's bound to be better than the average brew, but make sure you enjoy the process too. If you're only going through the steps to enjoy the place the steps lead to, it will be hard to really put in the effort the process requires. If you focus so much on the destination that the journey is just a series of steps you take, then the payoff at the end will be diminished significantly. Enjoy every part of your tea, making and drinking. If you want to be miserable, complain about cleaning everything up after you're done. It's such a pain to get a sponge into an infuser.

# *Chapter Review*

- The process to make the tea can be simple, exhaustive, or a pleasant blend of the two
- If you want your tea to take time and effort, there is a vast array of apparatus and additives you can avail yourself to
- If you mostly just want a good drink but are willing to put some effort in, there are some primary steps and tools you'll want to use
- If you just want a hot drink, go to a hotel coffee bar, grab the first bag you see that says "tea," and toss it into some boiling water and call it a day
- This chapter explores the step-by-step process of making a cup of Earl Grey
- While the content of the steps may vary from tea to tea, the actions themselves should remain consistent
- Step 1: Select your leaf - loose leaf of high quality is best for Earl Grey because you will be able to see the actual bergamot peels and know the flavor is genuine and full
- Step 2: Make a blend - If you want to enhance the flavor before you brew, add some dry ingredients to the mix. Lavender and vanilla are common for Earl Grey
- Step 3: Gather apparatus - temperature controlled kettle, infuser with narrow holes, a decanter to keep your liquid sweeteners organized, a narrow spoon for maximum stirring potential, a cup, and a saucer that doesn't throw the cup willy nilly

- Step 4: Steep - leave your tea untouched in the cup or pot for exactly as long as you're supposed to. A cursory search should tell you everything you need to know about tea times. For Earl Grey and most black teas, you'll want to leave the infuser in for 3-5 minutes, depending on the strength of the brew you're looking for.
- Step 5: Add flavors - sugars first, so they fully dissolve, then creams. Be careful with the ratios and experiment as much as you want. Pay attention to the color of the tea when you like it because that will make it much easier to repeat the process
- Step 6: Drink it - You have tea. Now drink it.

# Chapter 9: Drink While Hot

## *So Many Wasted Cups*

I like to drink tea while I work. I like the steam from my cup drifting by an illuminated computer screen. I like the smell of the tea, giving some connection to the real world as I work for hours on a computer screen where nothing feels completely real. I like the heat from my mug, reminding me that even pleasant things have urgency.

I also leave in my wake a growing horde of cold cups of tea. For every cup I successfully brew and drink, there is another on a bookshelf or still in my kitchen cooling alone and untended to. If cups of tea were children, I would be arrested for neglect.

Even while writing this final chapter, if I look to my left, I'll see a cat annoyed that she hasn't been given a second dinner, and next to her is a long-abandoned cup of jasmine tea. In everything I do, I leave behind a steady supply of cold teacups haunting me with their lost potential.

If the chapters of this book have made one point, it's that a lot can go into making a good cup of tea. Not all of it is essential. In fact, very little of it is. You can make a perfectly serviceable cup of tea with some hot water and the right dried plants, and nothing else. However, this book seeks to explore how to make a great cup of tea, so we get to delve into every facet of tea craft, down to the most minute, seemingly inconsequential detail.

With all that covered, there are only a few things left to consider as you make your tea—chief among them is to drink it while it's hot. Or, if you aren't making hot tea, then drink it when it's ready.

We have looked at all the minute steps that can go into making tea, how to flavor it, change it, brew it, and move it, and all that is to show that tea can take time, so you should take time for it. If you've gone through all that trouble of making the perfect cup of tea, whether that's an involved process of measuring loose-leaf or just throwing a bag in a cup, you should take some time to enjoy it. The investment of time tea merits does not end once the tea has finished brewing.

The reason I leave behind so many spoiled cups of cold tea is that I fail to take the time to enjoy them. I make them, get invested in the process of making them, then once the making is done, I haven't given myself time to enjoy them.

So if you take nothing else from the tips and lessons in this text, let it be to enjoy the tea you make and to make sure you have time to enjoy it.


## *But Wait, There's More*

Tea is a varied drink steeped in nuance and diversity, and with that comes a whole host of miscellaneous tips and hints for brewing the perfect cup for you. As much as this text has tried to categorize the entire process of making tea, some parts of it resist categorization, so we're left with some rogue tips.

Below are skills and tricks that resisted categorization and are just going to live as a bit of a bonus round.

**Tip #73: Do not attempt to use a coffee filter as a makeshift teabag. Coffee filters are a little thicker than tea bags so that the water won't penetrate quite as well. It should also be noted that coffee filters are shaped roughly like a small bowl, which is far different from a bag without extensive editing.**

**Tip #74: While tempting, pearl teas like Jasmine pearl are not the convenient portable teas they seem to be. When I was an optimistic grad student, I briefly carried a little tube of Jasmine pearls so I could plop one into a convenient cup of hot water if I encountered one. I did not realize that fishing the spidery tea out of my cup before it got bitter would be difficult, and I ended up with a scorched finger and a class full of very amused students.**

**Tip #75: If you spill honey onto yourself, a little hot water will get most of it out. If you, like me, hate to feel like your hands are dirty, getting a little honey on yourself can seem like a death sentence, but a quick trip to the restroom and some hot water can usually get honey off of you. Honey is sugar-based, and sugar is quick to dissolve in hot water. If it can dissolve in tea, it can probably dissolve in hot water. Just be careful not to burn yourself.**

**Tip #76:** If you like your sugar in cube form, be sure to keep it in an airtight container, not the cheap paper box it tends to be sold in. On one occasion, I returned to my office to find a legion of ants had made a sort of gluttonous castle out of my sugar cubes, and it took me about half a year before I could look at sugar cubes the same way again. If you use sugar in a packet, you have less to worry about, but I'd still recommend keeping an eye out for enterprising insects.

**Tip #77:** Wherever you drink tea most, keep a few boxes or blends that you don't necessarily favor. Some lovely friendships have been started over a shared cup of tea, and discovering that you have someone's favorite tea on hand is a unique pleasure. I like to keep about 30 different boxes in my office and pantry, even though I only regularly drink about 15 of them.

**Tip #78:** Store your tea in a cool, dry place away from direct sunlight. While tea cannot "go bad" per se, it can lose a lot of its flavor. Many teas get their flavor from special treatment in the leaves, and those flavors are delicate and can erode in the sun. You may think you're about to have a delicious cup only to find it bland, a shadow of its former glory.

**Tip #79:** Most tea bags are designed to flavor about 8 fl oz of water. If you notice that your tea is consistently weak or bland, check the size of the cup you're making it in. Instead of measuring my water every time, I prefer to use similarly sized cups when making my tea. In the past, when I've noticed my tea is a bit weak, I've realized that the cup I'm making it in is simply too big. Even a difference of a few ounces can make the tea taste weaker. I also like to purchase my teapots only if their volume is in multiples of 8 to make it easier to decide how many bags I need to flavor them.

Tip #80: If you are carrying loose leaf tea with you, make sure it is adequately labeled. Some teas, particularly mint, can be mistaken for certain illegal substances. It is a very awkward conversation with law enforcement when they find a bag of mysterious green herbs mixed with another mysterious crushed white powder. Explaining that it's just a baggie of your favorite travel tea with a crushed sugar cube will only get you so far. Luckily, mint has a smell that is easy to identify.

Tip #81: Tea is consumed almost everywhere in the world, so a tea shop is a perfect place to visit wherever you travel. You will find that the teas and merchandise may be different, but they tend to feel related. Though some tea shops will focus on the ceremony around tea, they are all still unified behind a shared love for tea, so it's worth checking in wherever you go.

Tip #82: Tea is a great souvenir if you are traveling. What could be better than to find the authentic taste of a new place? Many countries have been perfecting their tea craft for thousands of years, so visiting is your one chance to sample that experience and get a little taste of history.

Tip #83: Some teas can make an excellent base for a creative cocktail. Fruit teas go well with clear alcohols, and black teas are stunning companions to darker liquors. If you do make yourself a tea cocktail, add the alcohol after the tea has finished steeping, and be responsible with your consumption. Tea is already such an intoxicating experience, so be careful what you add to it.

Tip #84: A tea tasting event is a great place to make new friends with a shared interest in tea. Many tea shops host tea tastings you can attend, and they're as delightful as they sound. Often, you'll be placed with a small group of similarly excited tea enthusiasts and given several labeled cups to sample over a few hours. It's a great way to learn about lovely new teas and blends while also invigorating your social life.

Tip #85: If you notice your bagged tea has a faint metallic flavor, check to see how it is sealed. Many tea bags are sealed with a staple, and for the most part, the taste is unnoticeable, but with more subtle teas, it becomes abundantly clear that you're drinking office supplies. If you want to salvage your stapled tea, remove the staple and replace it with a tightly wound string. Be careful to ensure the bag is still sealed because many teabags contain finely ground tea that will escape through the smallest hole.

**Tip #86:** Many popular restaurants, including cafe chains, add sugar to their tea drinks without telling you. If you find that you cannot replicate a drink made for you at a chain even though you've bought the type of tea they use, try adding more sugar than you think is wise. Failing that, add more of the tea flavor and a bit of simple syrup.

**Tip #87:** Keep your tea away from your pets unless you're sure there's no risk. Some teas use herbs and flowers that can be poisonous to animals, so make sure they don't encounter one of your resting cups or the spent leaves from your infuser. That being said, catnip tea has the exact effect you would expect on cats, and mine flock to me whenever I drink it.

**Tip #88:** You can technically brew tea in already-flavored water; it just might taste odd. I have been known to make mint tea in cucumber water, and the result (when iced) is highly refreshing and a little surprising at the first sip. However, if the water is too saturated with flavor already, the tea will not steep as easily.

**Tip #89:** Many countries have specific foods and desserts that they consume with their tea, and if you ever get the chance, you should absolutely follow suit. Take a hint from people who have been honing their tea craft for years and enjoy it how they do, just to give it a chance. You will likely find something new to enjoy, and if you don't, there's always another cup.

Tip #90: A cup of black tea can be just as strongly caffeinated as a cup of coffee, so be careful if you're drinking it before bed, or be informed if you're drinking it to wake up. A single cup of coffee generally has anywhere from 70 - 95 mg of caffeine. A cup of black tea can have anywhere from 45 - 80 mg. If you mix your tea with any name-brand energy drink, you will get a concoction that is as energizing as it is terrible.

Tip #91: Some teas smell more enticing than they taste, so sample every part of the tea before you buy it in bulk. On a few occasions, I have purchased loose leaf tea in bulk that I had not tried before. When I took it home, I made my first cup and was treated to what I call "guest tea" because it's the tea I'll offer to guests if it happens to be their favorite. Try a cup of the tea you intend to buy. It adds a new layer to the investment, and you won't end up with a shelf full of rooibos that tastes like the most pungent, herbal shoes you'll ever find.

Tip #92: There are many things you can do to enhance the experience of drinking tea, and music is a great place to start! I like to listen to certain types of music paired with certain teas to build a kind of double association. Classical music goes great with English breakfast, but I might be alone in thinking heavy metal goes with Oolong.

Tip #93: If you are working on getting in shape or losing weight, tea is a great way to do it, but not in the way you might expect. Some teas do increase your metabolism slightly, which can help, but tea is also a low or no-calorie drink that is delicious any time of day. Drink a cup with your meals, and you'll notice your portion sizes can be smaller because you've filled up on delicious, delicious tea.

Tip #94: Avoid mixing too many teas. When I was young and full of hubris, I endeavored to combine every herbal tea I could find in one giant pot (it was a bucket) of tea. I think I added 11 different types of tea to the mix. What I expected was either the most healthy beverage known to man or for a portal to open and a demon to drag me into it for my arrogance. What I got was a medicinal bucket full of lukewarm water. It tasted like a wet cough drop.

Tip #95: For a fun tea game, cross out everything but the brewing time from your tea label and try to guess which tea it is. You may be surprised that by going in blind, you will experience the tea differently, and it can be fun to play with other tea lovers.

Tip #96: If you're bringing tea with you when you're camping or out in the wild, consider one with properties that can improve your digestion if something in the outdoors doesn't agree with you.

Tip #97: If you are sharing a romantic night out with another tea lover, it is said that red ginseng is a powerful aphrodisiac. The flavor is strong and sharp, and the experience of drinking it is something you can share with someone special.

Tip #98: Tea can be used as a flavor in baking! You can use the infused water from tea to replace the water in some baking recipes and give your treats a marvelous tea flavor.

Tip #99: There is tea for everything, every occasion, and food pairing. If you have a craving, you can most likely find a tea to suit it. There is even chocolate tea!

Tip #100: If you are leaving your tea to steep, leave it somewhere you can see without turning. It's easy to forget about your tea and get drawn back into whatever you were doing.

# *Chapter Review*

- Tea takes time to make well, so you should take time to enjoy it.
- Drink your tea while it's hot.
- Or just drink your tea when it's ready.
- Many other miscellaneous tips can help you make a good cup of tea, and this chapter includes them and some additional fun bonuses. Tea is a variable drink, so there will always be something new for you to learn and try. Experiment and enjoy the process of that experimentation.

# Chapter 10: Enjoy

## *Thank You for Learning about Tea with Me*

Tea is one of my favorite things in the world, and if you share that sentiment, then it should be comforting to know just how much company you have. Tea is beloved around the world. It earned that spot as water's only competition.

Tea means quite a lot to me. When I first started drinking tea in earnest, it was after breaking from a rather significant addiction to coffee. According to my doctor, I was drinking too much coffee. Too much, by her definition, was over 5 cups a day for someone my age. I often strayed into the range of 20 cups a day, and my body was grumpy for it. The worst part was that I wasn't even good at making coffee. I could almost understand my reliance on the stuff if I liked it, but nobody told me that you don't have to fill the coffee filter completely, so I just thought the coffee you made at home was supposed to be terrible. Why else would there be so many coffee shops if not actually to enjoy it once in a while?

My body wasn't working too well with that much coffee running through it, not to mention the other bad decisions someone young and in college will make with their body (pancakes were my other vice of choice). So I turned to tea. I needed something that still had a little caffeine, and tea is often almost as strong as coffee, so I gave it a try.

And I was hooked for life.

For many people, tea is part of their culture. It's tied intrinsically with some of the most critical facets of their life. For others, tea is both a formal event and a beloved staple of the day. Tea has many faces. It can do what it wants.

Tea is important.

And if you've read this far, tea is probably important to you too and isn't it nice knowing how large of a community you live in. The global populace seems at first to share so few things, but one thing you can pretty much rely on is tea. Wherever you go, you can land at a teahouse and find a friendly face and a familiar brew.

And as you travel and meet new people, pay attention to the teas they love and the way they make and drink them. Like cooking, making tea is a shared process. Take what you learn home with you and see how you can change the familiar and make it something new. As much as chain cafes represent a problem in consumerism, they did take something that existed in the world and cater it to the audience in the room. The Starbucks chai is the perfect example of this. Masala Chai is often very spicy, with a kick that is mellowed only by the milk and cream it is brewed in. Starbucks popularized a much, much sweeter form of the chai, to the point that to some people, the drink may be unrecognizable, but that's how everything works.

Food travels and changes. Fashion morphs to fit the preferences of the people who wear it. Language grows to fit the needs of the people who use it. As important and culturally essential as it is, tea is allowed to change for people who want it to change.

See what makes other teas different, learn from it, and see if you can make something different too.

This text has covered a lot of ground. As a refresher, we discussed:

## *What Kinds of Tea are Out There?*

Green, black, white, herbal, oolong, and so many more teas populate the world's cups and pots. Categorizing tea is difficult because every time you think you've managed to pin it down, you find another type of tea, and the people who brew it have been doing it for a thousand years, so it's not new, just new to you. Tea is as variable as the people who drink it, and that's what makes it exciting. Through a shared love of tea, you both have something in common with people worldwide, but you also have your local twist to it.

## *What Does Tea Look Like When You Make It?*

Generally, when you brew your tea, it will either be in a bag, a sachet, or an infuser. If your tea is in a bag, then there is a chance it has been ground, but that also means it will likely brew fast and strong. If it's in a sachet, that means you can probably expect more whole leaves that will expand and diffuse in the water, but sachets are also quite delicate. If it's in an infuser, that means you've got loose leaf tea. Loose leaf tea doesn't come prepackaged, and it's left to you to measure it out yourself, which is intimidating, but it also means you can customize it more than you could with other forms of tea. Infusers are what you use when you want to steep loose leaf tea. They're often metal cages you fill with tea that will sink in your cup or pot and allow each leaf to expand and release its flavor.

## *What Do You Need to Brew Your Tea?*

At its most simple, the only things you need to make tea are hot water, something to put it in, and tea. However, if you want to make consistently good tea, there are some things you'll want. You'll need a precise water heater, a good cup, the right-sized teapot made of a good heat resistant material, and you'll need tea. If you're using loose leaf tea, there's even more you'll want to get. An infuser is a standard tool for brewing tea, and it's going to be an essential partner to your loose leaf teas. You can safely brew your loose leaf tea with an infuser without getting the leaves mixed into your cup or pot. There's even more, you can get to make the perfect cup of tea, including special apparatus for honey, but the basics are a good place to start.

# What Can You Add to Your Tea?

So much! You can add so many wonderful things to your tea to make the flavors come alive. If we simplify tea additives, we can characterize them as creams, sweeteners, citrus, and auxiliary flavors, but there's more than just that. Expand your tea horizons and investigate complimentary flavors for your favorite teas. The only limit is what you can get your hands on.

# What Can You Add to Your Tea Before You Even Brew It?

With loose leaf tea, you can make blends of tea and other flavors. Add spices, herbs, citrus flavors, or even other teas to complement the flavors of your brew before you even expose it to the water. You can do the same thing with bagged tea, but it's a little more involved. You can make a blend of the flavors you want to complement your tea with. Put them somewhere safe and airtight, likely a jar. Then, fill an infuser whenever you brew the tea you want to flavor and add the infuser along with the bag. You'll have your own little blend in separate parts.

# What are the Rules of Tea?

There are no hard and fast rules for tea, and even tea etiquette is only really followed in formal settings. However, if you want to follow tea etiquette, you can investigate the rules and traditions related to the tea in your area. Tea is consumed all around the world, and with that comes a wildly diverse array of rules for drinking it, so there's no one hard and fast set of rules for drinking tea.

## *What Kinds of Mistakes Do People Make?*

All kinds! But also none. If you like the tea you make, then you haven't made a mistake, but if you're looking to change how you make your tea and improve it from a technical standpoint, then there are a lot of little things people mess up. At every stage of the brewing process, there are decisions to be made and errors to be discovered. Before you brew your tea, you can select the wrong leaves, let the water get too hot, or heat it unevenly. Once your tea is steeping, you could leave it in too long or take it out too early. Even while you're drinking it, you could make the mistake of adding too much other flavoring and drown the delicate flavors of your tea. With so much that can happen, it's worth taking a moment to be careful and practice until you have a tea you love.

## *When Should You Drink Your Tea?*

When it's ready, you made something, and you made it for a reason. Enjoy it. Sit down with your tea, take a sip, and just live in that moment. Tea is a plant, a drink, and it's an experience. Enjoy it when it's ready to be enjoyed.

**Tip #101:** There is always more to learn about tea. If you love tea, you'll love more tea than you know about, so visit local tea shops and find new teas to enjoy.

# About the Expert

Jessica Kanzler lives in the United States with her wife and cats. She has been drinking tea ever since coffee betrayed her in college, and she has never once looked back. Jessica's love for tea has driven her to obsess about the stuff to the point that passion has become a full-time infatuation. Jessica's favorite tea is Earl Grey, followed closely by Jasmine. She prefers her tea hot, her cups deep, and her company generally silent and about 40 feet away. Beyond her obsession with tea, Jessica also writes freelance with a specialty in technology and pop culture, and she is also a director for a literacy-focused nonprofit.

HowExpert publishes quick 'how to' guides on all topics from A to Z by everyday experts. Visit HowExpert.com to learn more.

# Recommended Resources

- HowExpert.com – Quick 'How To' Guides on All Topics from A to Z by Everyday Experts.
- HowExpert.com/free – Free HowExpert Email Newsletter.
- HowExpert.com/books – HowExpert Books
- HowExpert.com/courses – HowExpert Courses
- HowExpert.com/clothing – HowExpert Clothing
- HowExpert.com/membership – HowExpert Membership Site
- HowExpert.com/affiliates – HowExpert Affiliate Program
- HowExpert.com/jobs – HowExpert Jobs
- HowExpert.com/writers – Write About Your #1 Passion/Knowledge/Expertise & Become a HowExpert Author.
- HowExpert.com/resources – Additional HowExpert Recommended Resources
- YouTube.com/HowExpert – Subscribe to HowExpert YouTube.
- Instagram.com/HowExpert – Follow HowExpert on Instagram.
- Facebook.com/HowExpert – Follow HowExpert on Facebook.

Made in the USA
Columbia, SC
09 July 2021

41610112R00067